# THE PSYCHOLOGY OF
# ARISTOTLE

NUMBER I OF THE
COLUMBIA STUDIES IN PHILOSOPHY
EDITED UNDER THE DEPARTMENT OF
PHILOSOPHY, COLUMBIA UNIVERSITY

# THE PSYCHOLOGY OF ARISTOTLE

## *An Analysis of the Living Being*

By CLARENCE SHUTE

*NEW YORK*
RUSSELL & RUSSELL · INC
1964

REISSUED, 1964, BY RUSSELL & RUSSELL, INC.
BY ARRANGEMENT WITH COLUMBIA UNIVERSITY PRESS
L. C. CATALOG CARD NO: 64—13937

Manufactured in the United States of America

*To*

*My Parents*

# FOREWORD

AFTER two thousand years the writings of Aristotle remain unexcelled as a field of investigation for the student of philosophy. So relevant are they to the persisting questions about the universe in which man finds himself that the interpretation of Aristotle has naturally been approached from many points of interest. He has thus been the intellectual master of movements differing widely in purpose and method, and the expositions of his writings have inevitably shown the results of these divergent claims.

The aim of the present study is not to discuss and to seek a solution for the questions which have arisen in the historic expositions of Aristotle's psychology. It is rather to follow the way in which Aristotle himself develops his treatment of behavior as one aspect—and that the most essential one—of living things in general. In the conviction that this is the way to a clear understanding of Aristotle's psychological doctrine, the writer heartily concedes that he is the child of his age and liable to the errors that any background of approach is likely to lead to. But with this difference: that the interest of contemporary thought, and especially of contemporary psychology, seems to be so close to that which inspired Aristotle, that the present study may, it is to be hoped, avoid questions which are non-Aristotelian in nature and focus attention on what is most germane to Aristotle's interpretation of living—especially of human living.

This study of the Aristotelian writings has led to an exposition characterized by two major emphases. First, it begins with the more general biological inquiries into generation and growth, because in the setting of this account of the individual's development it becomes much clearer what Aristotle meant by ψυχή than if a beginning were made with his treatment of the individual's matured powers. Second, the theme of the importance of the organism's environment, which is suggested in the opening chapters on development, swells to complete dominance of the entire field, so that behavior is seen to be interpreted entirely in terms of interaction between the organism and the environing world. The accentuation of this pattern, as the essay proceeds, is a reflection of the way in which it becomes increasingly the controlling principle as the higher levels of life are considered.

If it appears to the reader that undue emphasis is placed upon these aspects of the treatment, he is asked to consider that it would not be profitable to present the mass of detail which has been studied in the original, translated into other languages, and commented upon for two thousand years. The present study seeks rather to present the fundamental pattern of Aristotle's psychology in bold outline, the details serving to illustrate how the central doctrine is applied to the specific fields of psychological inquiry.

I am indebted to Professor John Herman Randall, Jr., of

Columbia University, for the suggestion which led to the study of Aristotle's psychological writings in their wider biological context. The friendly counsel which made available to me the wealth of Professor Randall's Aristotelian scholarship and the painstaking criticism by which he enabled me to clarify my exposition are responsible for the success which I trust the essay achieves in exhibiting the central argument of Aristotle's psychology. My interest in this subject is continuous with my general psychological study, in which field I pay tribute to the late Professor Joseph Peterson, of George Peabody College for Teachers. His devotion to rigorous scientific method and his serene confidence in living were worthy of the emulation of every student. Finally, I gratefully acknowledge my profound debt to the late Dean Woodbridge, of Columbia University. His awakening lectures, his incisive discussions, and his generous personal counsel were large factors in the directing and sharpening of my thought, and I shall be glad if this essay, in a field of inquiry which was a central interest in his philosophy, manifests to some degree the extent of his influence.

C. S.

Lake Erie College
Painesville, Ohio
July, 1941

# CONTENTS

# ABBREVIATIONS

Bekker's Greek text, Berlin, 1831, is the principal standard of reference for subsequent work. Below are listed modern revised texts and convenient translations. Quotations in the body of the essay are from these works, the pagination being that of Bekker's text.

Ph, *Physica*. Text revised and translated by P. H. Wicksteed and F. M. Cornford, Loeb Classical Library, Harvard University Press.

Dgc, *De generatione et corruptione*. Text revised and translated by H. H. Joachim, Clarendon Press, Oxford.

Me, *Metaphysica*. Text revised and translated by H. Tredennick, Loeb Classical Library, Harvard University Press.

Dpa, *De partibus animalium*. Translated by W. Ogle, Clarendon Press, Oxford. Based on Bekker's text revised by the translator.

Dma, *De motu animalium*. Translated by A. S. L. Farquharson, Clarendon Press, Oxford. Based on Bekker's text revised by the translator.

Dga, *De generatione animalium*. Translated by A. Platt, Clarendon Press, Oxford. Based on Bekker's text revised by the translator.

Ha, *Historia animalium*. Translated by D'Arcy W. Thompson, Clarendon Press, Oxford. Based on Bekker's text revised by the translator.

Da, *De anima.*

Dss, *De sensu et sensibili.*

Dmr, *De memoria et reminiscentia.*

Dsv, *De somno et vigilia.*

Ds, *De somniis.* Text revised and translated by W. S. Hett, Loeb Classical Library, Harvard University Press.

EN, *Ethica Nicomachea.* Text revised and translated by H. Rackham, Loeb Classical Library, Harvard University Press.

Grateful acknowledgment is made to the Clarendon Press, Oxford, and to the Harvard University Press for permission to quote from these translations of the works of Aristotle.

C. S.

*Chapter One*

# THE GENERATION OF THE ORGANISM

OF THINGS constituted by nature some are ungenerated, imperishable, and eternal, while others are subject to generation and decay. The former are excellent beyond compare and divine, but less accessible to knowledge. . . . Both departments, however, have their special charm. The scanty conceptions to which we can attain of celestial things give us, from their excellence, more pleasure than all our knowledge of the world in which we live; just as a half-glimpse of persons that we love is more delightful than a leisurely view of other things, whatever their number and dimensions. On the other hand, in certitude and in completeness our knowledge of terrestrial things has the advantage. . . . Having already treated of the celestial world, as far as our conjectures could reach, we proceed to treat of animals, without omitting, to the best of our ability, any member of the kingdom, however ignoble. For if some have no graces to charm the sense, yet even these, by disclosing to intellectual perception the artistic spirit that designed them, give immense pleasure to all who can trace links of causation, and are inclined to philosophy. . . . Absence of haphazard and conduciveness of everything to an end are to be found in Nature's works in the highest degree, and the resultant end of her generations and combinations is a form of the beautiful. If any person thinks the examination of the rest of the animal kingdom an unworthy task. he must hold in like disesteem the study of man [Dpa, 644b, f.].

A great deal of Aristotle's natural philosophy is epitomized in this beautiful passage. Man, as a member of the kingdom of animals, is part of the natural order which is subject to generation and decay. But these natural objects which are less excellent and divine do nevertheless exhibit a structure of significance to the philosopher, the study of which will please while it instructs. In the very definition of this class of things we are introduced at once to the serious problem presented by the apparent fact of genesis.

In the doctrines of the monists and pluralists who preceded Aristotle there was no room for any such natural process. For the monists, all reality was one, and there could therefore be no genuine coming-to-be, but only alteration of properties. Although Anaxagoras, in what Aristotle criticized as a position inconsistent with his pluralism, identified coming-to-be and passing-away with alteration, as did the monists, Leucippus and Democritus attributed the phenomenon to the association and dissociation of unchanging constituent elements. These earlier philosophers were attempting through closer analysis to get behind what previously had been taken as real coming-to-be; but Aristotle, attacking the problem with a broader appreciation of the observed character of natural processes, found the need to be rather for a truer account of the factors involved in a genuine coming-to-be and passing-away than for the identification of these processes with either alteration or association and dissociation.

We may say that Aristotle believed neither that there was one substance, as did the monists, nor that there was one kind of substance in the sense of the atomists. What we find naturally existing are concrete wholes which embrace "in a single complex a diversity of constituent elements, factors, or properties" (Ph, 184a). In this view of nature there is not only room for true coming-to-be, but it is indeed encountered as a basic type of natural change. For what we actually see are these concrete wholes which are so diversified; and certain of the changes which are presented to our observation cannot be explained satisfactorily as other than the coming-to-be and passing-away of these things, as distinct from mere alteration or association and dissociation.

Plato's treatment of this subject was not satisfactory to Aristotle. Plato had, indeed, given it his attention, but his failure to discuss alteration and growth as other forms of change made the treatment incomplete. Perhaps still more antagonistic to Aristotle's thought was Plato's confining of his discussion to the coming-to-be of the elements alone, neglecting to give answers to the various questions of how such compound things as flesh or bones come-to-be. For while Aristotle is always dealing with fundamental principles, he is interested in them only as they are found to be the explanation of concrete things.

In Aristotle's doctrine there are two aspects of the general problem of development: first, how the organism is initiated; and second, how the generated organism develops into its mature form. There is a sense in which these two branches of the investigation are fundamentally one, for even a perfect embryo is not yet a perfect animal (Dga, 737b). In coming-to-be, the organism does not spring from nothing or from unrelated causes; in a similar way, at any subsequent stage of development there is a determinate relation between the present state of the organism and its previous history.

## DISTINCTIONS INVOLVED IN THE EXPLANATION OF GENERATION

In Aristotle's analysis of coming-to-be and passing-away there are involved certain characteristic ways of stating the traits of his subject matter. The first of these is the doctrine to which allusion has been made, that concrete, particular, whole things are the starting point for the investigations of the natural philosopher. The "whole" depends for its existence upon the elements into which it can be analyzed, but it cannot be understood in terms of these elements alone. Therefore it was an error, Aristotle said, to suppose that "coming-to-be and passing-away in the unqualified and complete sense" (as distinct from coming to be "such" or "so much") could be described in terms of association and dissociation of elements alone, while alteration was the proper term to describe change in what was continuous. On the contrary, unqualified coming-to-be and passing-away

> take place when a thing changes, from *this* to *that*, as a whole. . . . For in that which underlies the change there is a factor corresponding to the definition and there is a material factor. When, then, the change is in these constitutive factors, there will be coming-to-be or passing-away: but when it is in the thing's qualities . . . [and only accidentally a change of the thing itself], there will be "alteration" [Dgc, 317a].

This is a rejection of the atomistic doctrine, which held that permanent elements persist through every change, and far from explaining true coming-to-be, merely explained it away. In the strongest terms Aristotle asserts that "when nothing persists, of which the resultant is a property (or an 'accident' in any sense of the term), it is 'coming-to-be,' and the converse change is 'passing-away' " (Dgc, 320a).

A further characteristic of these concrete things, which is significant not only in the generation but in the entire history of an organism, is that their existence and activity always involve determinate relations to their environmental context and cannot be adequately understood apart from them. In chapter v of *De motu animalium* Aristotle recognizes "that which causes its own qualitative changes, and its own growth"; yet later he declares that nothing can "possibly be the cause of its own generation and decay, for the mover must exist before the moved, the begetter before the begotten, and nothing is prior to itself" (Dma, 700a, b). We shall find, then, that in one sense the organism is acting autonomously; in another it is the locus of factors which cannot be identified with it (even if they cannot be abstracted from it), which are the causes of its generation and decay.

Natural philosophy takes account of both these sets of conditions, and relates them all to the form as a whole. For while Aristotle laid the greatest stress on extensive investigations of the parts of natural objects, it was because of his interest in their integration rather than in the parts themselves (Dpa, 645a). This constitutes the field in which moves his extended discussion of coming-to-be and passing-away, found principally in *De generatione et corruptione* and *Physica*.

These phenomena of coming-to-be and passing-away appear as a passage from the potential into the actual—a kind of change which is operative also throughout the process of development.

In one sense things come-to-be out of that which has no "being" without qualification: yet in another sense they come-to-be always out of "what is." For coming-to-be necessarily implies the pre-existence of something which *potentially* "is," but *actually* "is not"; and this something is spoken of both as "being" and as "not being" [Dgc, 317b].

The fact that Aristotle accepted what is called "spontaneous generation" as the way in which some organisms come-to-be shows that with regard to these organisms he considered that appropriate material for their generation could both exist and be changed into their living forms by stimulation other than that coming from the activity of like organisms. But in the case of living things which are at all analogous to man, in whom we are primarily interested, he believed them to come-to-be only when appropriate material furnished by a member of a species is organized by a begetter of the same or closely related species.

In discussing the generation of organisms we must keep in mind that the material to which reference is made is not mere indeterminate matter or an aggregation of the four elements. This material occupies a position intermediate between such matter and the organism which will be generated, with determinate potentialities for change in either of two directions. In discussing combination Aristotle says that "the compound may *be-actually* other than the constituents from which it has resulted; nevertheless each of them may still *be-potentially* what it was before they were combined, and both of them may survive undestroyed" (Dgc, 327b). This material has therefore the possibility of separation into its constituents. On the other hand, it has the possibility of becoming a new organism when the principle of movement is imparted to it. That this was Aristotle's view is shown in his discussion of the female contribution to generation, since this contribution was the material for the future organism, informed only by a potential nutritive soul: "The real cause why each of them [i. e., the parts] comes into being is that the secretion of the female is potentially such as the animal is naturally, and all the parts are potentially present in it, but none actually" (Dga, 740b).

Few things are more essential to the whole Aristotelian view of nature than this doctrine of the passage from the potential to the actual. It first insists on the basic conditions of all change, which the mechanical view of natural processes singles out for exclusive attention. That is, Aristotle recognizes continuity of natural process and the presence of necessary antecedents. It is impossible to have *this* without *that.* One phenomenon does not spring full-grown into the world of things without being brought there in due form according to the rules. So far he agrees with the mechanist.

He then passes beyond the mechanist in offering what the latter cannot produce—a reasonable explanation for the appearance of *new* things. If anything is evident in nature, from the processes of metabolism in organisms too small for Aristotle's eye to observe, to the processes of human thinking, it is the coming into being of that which before was not. The mechanist reduces these processes to mechanical combinations. The dualist postulates an additional separable factor to account for what, to him, is clearly beyond the province of the mechanical. In contrast to both,

Aristotle takes as his starting point the indisputable fact that certain objects which he is to investigate act "by nature" rather than in other ways, and coming-to-be is one of these observable activities which occur by nature. For natural processes are the kind of behavior which can be understood in terms of principles which reside in the behaving thing itself, and these principles embrace a set of determinate possibilities which are the basis for the process of new things' coming-to-be—always remembering that these principles can be further defined as characteristic ways of responding to external stimuli (Ph, Book II, chap. i).

Just what Aristotle means by coming-to-be and the passage from the potential to the actual is further clarified in his placing the field of coming-to-be and passing-away in that of contraries and their intermediates. It appears that the analysis aims to exhibit certain distinctions which can usefully be made in terms of contraries and of action and passion, without necessarily implying that this usage is entirely uniform with that which is made of these terms in treating the other three fundamental kinds of change, through which an οὐσία obviously persists. In *Physica*, Book I, chapter vii, he distinguishes in the complex thing that "becomes" two elements: one is that which begins to exist, and this is the new "form"; the second is what takes on this form. In the case of the latter it is evident that there is something which persists through the developmental change, and also the aggregate of qualities of this persisting subject which move along the line between two antitheses. In stating the matter thus, as the context shows, Aristotle had in mind qualified coming-to-be (or coming-to-be *such*) rather than unqualified. In the above quotations from *De generatione et corruptione* (317a, 320a) it is clear that unqualified coming-to-be involves change in both the material and the form, so that nothing perceptible persists except the form, and that in a generic sense only.

In *De generatione et corruptione* this view is based on the nature of action and passion. There (324a) it is asserted that "since (a) patient and agent are generically identical (i. e., 'like') but specifically 'unlike,' [e. g., two men, as such, are generically like, while as individuals they are specifically unlike] while (b) it is 'contraries' that exhibit this character: it is clear that 'contraries' and their 'intermediates' are such as to suffer action and to act reciprocally—for indeed it is these that constitute the entire sphere of passing-away and coming-to-be."

In *Physica* (Book I, chapter vii) it is shown that the two contraries can be considered as one quality and the absence of this quality, respectively, just as in the same work he asserts that existence and nonexistence are the limiting terms of coming-to-be and passing-away (261a). This passage may be considered together with a further one from *De generatione et corruptione:* "For agent and patient are contrary to one another, and coming-to-be is a process into the contrary: hence the patient *must* change into the agent, since it is only thus that coming-to-be will be a process into the contrary" (324a). Assuming the consistency of the two passages, the implication is that, whatever the agent proves to be, the patient is, in a sense, the absence of this agent. This is another way of saying that in unqualified genesis the only contraries which are observable are the presence and absence of a given kind of thing, as distinct from the presence and absence of involved material.

Now in the coming-to-be of an organism, what is the agent, and what is the patient? ". . . it is no doubt true . . . that one thing 'comes-to-be' (in the unqualified sense) out of another thing: and further it is true that the efficient cause of its coming-to-be is either (i) an actual thing (which is the same as the effect either *generically*—for the efficient cause of the coming-to-be of a hard thing is not a hard thing—or *specifically,* as e. g., fire is the efficient cause of the coming-to-be of fire or one man of the birth of another), or (ii) an actuality" (Dgc, 320b). In the case of an organism it may be confidently stated that Aristotle conceived the efficient cause under both of these aspects. In the above reference he cites as an example of the efficient cause as an actual thing, specifically the same as the effect, one man as the efficient cause of the birth of another. On the other hand he says that the soul may be defined as "the first actuality of a natural body potentially possessing life" (Da, 412a), which identifies the soul with the second kind of thing which can be an efficient cause. We shall see from our later discussion of Aristotle's causes, as they are applied biologically, that the soul is indeed considered to be an efficient cause of an organism's coming-to-be. Yet in this conceiving of the soul as an efficient cause in generation it is not as something apart from the begetter, but rather as that which constitutes the nature of the begetter (Ph, 198a), the efficient cause being not two, but one considered in two different ways.

If in this sense (viz., that it is only through a begetter characterized by a given form that there will come-to-be another thing of like form) the soul is the agent in begetting —the agent of the passage between contraries, one of which is the agent itself—what then is the patient? There can be, apparently, only one answer: the patient is the appropriate material which has the power to receive this form, but actually is devoid of it.

This conclusion has far-reaching consequences which we shall have further occasion to consider in our study of the individual. To summarize, we have so far found that in things constituted by nature different materials have appropriate potentialities for receiving specific forms; in the domain of living things the actualization of these potentialities by the activity of a begetter, contributing the principle of movement, is what we mean by unqualified coming-to-be of concrete things; this process of genesis, as is the case with all other processes of living, takes place according to principles which are appropriate to and reside in the things themselves; each thing is actually what it is and potentially that into which it will develop; this passage of the potential into the actual in the positive direction is accomplished by an efficient cause which can be regarded under two aspects which are inseparable: a begetter, and the factor of "soul" characterizing the begetter. On the one hand, a wholly unformed, inert matter has not been brought into life by the imparting of a certain pattern, for the matter involved was already "formed" in a way appropriate for the coming-to-be of the new; on the other hand, a separable soul has not come into matter, or become related to matter, to produce the result. There has been a movement in the sphere of nature (which is "the distinctive form or quality of such things as have within themselves a principle of motion, such form or characteristic property not being separable from the things themselves, save conceptually" [Ph, 193b]) whereby a new concrete thing has been actualized from the potential.

### THE SENSES IN WHICH PSYCHE IS A FACTOR IN GENERATION

Our present study is concerned with Aristotle's doctrine of human living, and it must be pointed out that no understanding of his psychology is possible apart from this biological starting point. The "psyche" of Aristotle must not be misunderstood as something separable or apart from natural processes. No living process can be thought of as devoid of psyche for it is the first principle of living things (Da, 420a). And, on the other hand, psyche must not be abstracted, for it is always immersed in matter.

To understand just what Aristotle means by psyche, or soul, in his specific discussion of biological generation requires a further examination of the four familiar "causes" which he distinguishes to explain the processes of nature: the final, formal, material, and efficient. On page 715a of *De generatione animalium* he says that we may consider the final cause and the formal cause as practically the same, while on page 724a, b, we read,

> Now the offspring comes *from* the semen, and . . . either the semen is the material from which it is made, or it is the first efficient cause. . . . We must discover, then, in which of the two other classes the semen is to be put, whether it is to be regarded as matter, and therefore acted upon by something else, or as a form, and therefore acting upon something else, or as both at once.

Here form becomes largely one with efficient cause. In a passage of *Physica* it is shown how the understanding of the four causes is important for the philosopher, although in operation three of them coincide.

Clearly, then, the "becauses" being such and so classified, it behoves the natural philosopher to understand all four, and to be able to indicate, in answer to the question "how and why," the material, the form, the moving force, and the goal or purpose, so far as they come within the range of Nature. But in many cases three of these "becauses" coincide; for the essential nature of a thing and the purpose for which it is produced are often identical (so that the final cause coincides with the formal), and moreover the efficient cause must bear some resemblance in "form" to the effect (so that the efficient cause too must, so far, coincide with the formal); for instance, man is begotten by man. And this applies universally to all things that cause motion and are themselves moved [Ph, 198a].

(It will be noted that while Aristotle says that the final and formal causes are often identical, the relationship between the formal and efficient is of a looser kind, viz., the efficient cause must resemble the effect in form; so that it is proper to say that in many cases the three coincide, not that they are identical.) We conclude from these passages that, in biology, the four factors become for practical purposes two: the material and psyche, which functions as the final, formal, and efficient causes; and it is quite evident that "parts" and "functions" (always specifically considered) are comprehensive terms under which Aristotle subsumes the conditions of development and experience.

The discussion of the relation between body and soul will be deferred to chapter v. Here it is necessary only to relate the more general question to the process of generation, a relation which can be expressed by saying that the body is made for the soul, the soul being thought of in its significance as final cause. It is clearly stated by Aristotle that since every instrument is for some purpose, and each of the parts of the body is for the sake of some form of action, so it is apparent that the body as a whole is organized for some total kind of behavior, just as sawing does not exist for the saw, but the saw for sawing. In like manner, the body is for the sake of the soul, and the parts for the functions for which they are made (Dpa, 645b). Further, soul is the agency by which the parts of the animal are made, or, in modern terminology, by which the parts of the animal are differentiated from the mass. "Either it is something external which makes them, or else something existing in the seminal fluid and the semen; and this must either be soul or a part of soul, or something containing soul" (Dga, 733b, f.).

In the above discussion two ideas may be distinguished. The soul functions in generation as final or formal cause; it also functions, through the action of the begetter, as efficient cause. Turning to *De anima,* we find the same view: it is explicitly stated that the soul functions as cause in three senses, which may roughly be classed as the final, the formal, and (as that which characterizes the begetter) the efficient. And finally, the soul is linked to development in general, not now as the soul of the begetter, but as the soul of the begotten:

> Change of state and growth are also due to the soul; for sensation is in a sense change of state, and nothing feels which has not a soul. The same is true about growth and decay [Da, 415b].

This soul of the begotten is definitely located in the body, beginning with the embryo, for otherwise something would be giving form to the body which was not in contact with it.

One of two things, then, must be necessary: the soul is in the embryo, either as a part of it or as separate from it, though internal. On the basis of the difficulties involved in the alternative, Aristotle pronounces for the soul's being a part of the whole animal, from its very beginning (Dga, 734a). This is the way we find the case stated in the text. Yet if we take into account other passages (e. g., the above citation from Dpa, 645b and others which will be considered when we come to analyze more closely what Aristotle means by soul), it would appear to represent Aristotle's view more accurately to speak of the soul characterizing the body, from the beginning of the embryo.

At this point we meet one of Aristotle's very interesting views—the distinction between the contributions in generation which are made by the male and female parents. The female alone furnishes the material, which is not mere matter but rather is such that it has determinate potentialities for receiving specific forms. But both are found to contribute to the soul of the embryo. This is definitely known from the fact that wind-eggs, though unfertilized, have life (for if they did not they could not rot—a provocative point in considering the potentialities of life) and therefore some soul potentially. This is nutritive soul, which is inadequate to differentiate the parts and perfect the animal without the male contribution, which includes sensitive soul as well as nutritive (Dga, 741a).

Granted that the female contributes nutritive soul, the distinction between the male and the female in generation is based on the distinction between soul as representing the final cause, the form, and the efficient cause, on the one hand, and body representing the material cause, on the other. In *De generatione animalium,* Book I, chapter ii, Aristotle describes the male and female principles as origins of generation, the former embodying the efficient cause, the latter the material. A functional definition of the two principles is given, making the male that which has the power to generate in another, while the female has the power to generate in itself.

Later (Book I, chapter xxi) Aristotle takes this distinction as an a priori argument (which he also seeks to confirm by facts) for the male's contributing only the power of movement in the embryo, not adding anything to the material. For "whenever one thing is made from two of which one is active and the other passive, the active agent does not exist in that which is made" (Dga, 729b).

Aristotle, working without the refined procedures available to the modern physiologist, found the female contribution to the embryo in the catamenia. In *De generatione animalium,* Book I, chapter xix, he discusses in detail the nature of the catamenia and their function in furnishing the matter to which form is given by the semen. Again and again, in this treatise, the principle is argued that the male contributes the active and the female the passive agent in generation; it is made just as plain, however, that the passive agent is such that the possibilities of being acted upon are strictly delimited.

### THE SIGNIFICANCE OF ARISTOTLE'S DOCTRINE OF DEVELOPMENT

All this is quite absorbing to the modern student, and he can see great error or great truth, or both, according as his interest leads him primarily into scientific detail or into underlying principles. Grant that the details concerning the differences between the male and female contributions to generation have to be ignored. The fact remains that Aristotle was reaching an underlying principle of abiding value, which modern investigations still find impossible to subsume under any more comprehensive principle. Why is it that four cells of an embryo, remaining united, develop into one individual and, divided into two groups, result in two individuals? Why is it that (in early stages) tissue transplanted from one part of an embryo to another will develop into a different part from what it would otherwise? Such questions were necessarily unknown to Aristotle. But his answer would have been in terms of the effect of the intimate environmental context on an embryo so characterized that it displays certain activity in such a context. The effect of this internal principle of movement can be observed, but it cannot in turn be explained through any further principle. In other words, a fundamental datum of the universe in which we live, regardless of whether the natural thing under consideration be a mature organism or an embryo, with which Aristotle was familiar, or the minutest unit of hereditary determination discovered by the latest technique, is activity which, while dependent upon material, employs this material as its instrument. Aristotle had penetrated with keen insight to the root of the problem of generation—how it is that a whole process takes place, which will eventually, through the processes we shall next examine, result in a highly differentiated and integrated organism—and his proposed solution was a repudiation of the materialists' hope to explain life completely in terms of the behavior of things as they act in nonliving contexts.

*Chapter Two*

# THE GROWTH OF THE ORGANISM

IN CHAPTER I we were engaged with the first aspect of the general problem of development—how a new organism comes to be. We turn next to examine the processes of growth, where we shall find that the major facts which concern us are more accessible to observation. This is not to say, however, that we shall be able to make a more ultimate analysis than in the former case. Here, as there, we come upon life process as something which, while dependent for its ongoing upon the presence of a definite kind of structure, cannot be understood in terms of structure alone.

Aristotle's discussion exhibits three kinds of activity involved in the growth of the initiated organism. Subject as it is, instantly, to the processes of degeneration, or katabolism, it must have that which will replenish its energy. As an organism which is only initiated, and only a small fraction of its effective size, there must be addition to its mass. Finally, it is a relatively homogeneous structure, from which must be differentiated and matured the parts that are necessary to carry on its characteristic activities. We shall call these three kinds of activity which are involved in the growth of the organism *nutrition, increase,* and *differentiation and maturation of the parts.*

Aristotle clearly distinguishes nutrition from the other aspects of growth (Dgc, 322a). The food which the organism receives has the power to become either flesh, or so-much flesh. In the first case the result is nutrition, in the second, growth. The latter process is thus something which is not merely the production of material, but of material related to a form which is undergoing change.

In one passage (Dpa, 647b) the difference between homogeneous and heterogeneous parts is discussed in a way which illustrates the further distinction between increase and differentiation. In some of the homogeneous parts, as the blood vessels, the same term serves to designate an entire part and a portion of that part. This is not the case with heterogeneous parts, such as the face, where the same term cannot be applied to the portion of a part which is applied to the whole. While Aristotle himself does not draw the parallel, this difference is similar to the difference which exists between increase and differentiation, for the growth of the organism involves not only its becoming more of the same kind of material, but its becoming differentiated in its organization.

This distinction between increase and differentiation is further noted in Aristotle's discussion of the nature of semen:

> . . . how will the foetus become greater by the addition of something else if that which is added remain unchanged? But if that which is added *can* change, then why not say that the semen from the very first is of such a kind that blood and flesh

can be made out of it [rather, *by its agency*], instead of saying that it itself *is* blood and flesh? [Dga, 723a].

The fetus is here shown to be something which does not merely increase in size by the accession of food; it uses this food to make something quite different from its original structure. The completion of this process is necessary before the generation of the organism, in its fullest sense, can be said to be complete (Dga, 737b).

### NUTRITION

Turning to investigate these three kinds of activities which are thus distinguished, we shall have little to say concerning nutrition. Obviously, the nutriment and that which it nourishes are quite different in character. Not only is something done to the nutriment, but the selection of the nutriment itself is determined by the character of that which is nourished. "And since that from which an organ comes into being and that by which it is increased are the same (i. e. the nutriment), each of the parts will be made out of such a material and such residual matter as it is able to receive" (Dga, 766a). It is significant that in this basic activity of nutrition we find Aristotle's analysis in terms of a thing-in-its-environment. The environment here furnishes the nutriment, without which the organism is helpless. Yet what happens to the nutriment, in turn, is determined by the character of the organism.

### INCREASE

When we come to consider increase as an activity involved in growth, we again meet the distinction between contraries which we found in the analysis of generation. Aristotle contrasts the various contraries as follows:

"When the change from contrary to contrary is *in quantity,* it is 'growth and diminution'; when it is *in place,* it is 'motion'; when it is in property, i. e. *in quality,* it is 'alteration'; but when nothing persists, of which the resultant is a property (or an 'accident' in any sense of the term), it is 'coming-to-be,' and the converse change is 'passing-away' " (Dgc, 319b, f.). The difference between the analysis into contraries in generation and the analysis into contraries in growth (as increase) can therefore be said to be this: in increase the contraries are the presence and absence of more of the same kind of thing; in generation the contraries are the presence and absence of that kind of thing itself.

There are three things which characterize the process of increase: ". . . (i) any and every part of the growing magnitude is made bigger (e. g. if flesh grows, every particle of the flesh gets bigger), (ii) by the accession of something, and (iii) in such a way that the growing thing is preserved and persists" (Dgc, 321a). The first of these distinctive marks of increase again suggests a comparison with generation. It is when a thing as a whole changes from *this* to *that,* that coming-to-be takes place. It is when a magnitude (which may not be the entire organism, to be sure) changes in quantity in every part that increase takes place. The second mark has to do with the mutual relationship between the organism and its environment which we have noticed above. The third distinguishes increase from nutrition, by which the thing is merely preserved but not increased; and from differentiation, in which the thing persists, indeed, but with the added factor of the actualization of the potential form.

This distinction between matter and form is used by

Aristotle to make clear the meaning of his statement that every part of a given magnitude is affected in the process of increase. The implications of this view seemed to Aristotle to lead to fallacious conclusions if one assumed that only matter was being talked about. The partially suppressed argument seems to be this: if every part of the matter grows by the accession of a body, and if the accession of a body is impossible without contact, then the presence of these acceding bodies within the growing matter would necessitate two bodies occupying the same space.

The difficulty involved in this statement of the case is overcome by distinguishing matter and form in the process of growth (as increase).

> We must note (i) that the organic parts grow by the growth of the tissues . . . and (ii) that flesh, bone, and every such part —like every other thing which has its form immersed in matter —has a twofold nature: for the form as well as the matter is called "flesh" or "bone."
>
> Now, that any and every part of the tissue *qua* form should grow—and grow by the accession of something—is possible, but not that any and every part of the tissue *qua* matter should do so [Dgc, 321b].

We are sorely tempted to accuse Aristotle of excusing himself from difficulties in one type of analysis by shifting to another as readily as the Clerk of Copmanhurst doffed his frock and Latin for the green and battle-ax. But before passing judgment let us examine a further elaboration of the same theme.

> Hence in one sense it is true that any and every part of the flesh has grown; but in another sense it is false. For there has been an accession to every part of the flesh in respect to its form, but not in respect to its matter. The whole, however, has become

larger. And this increase is due (a) on the one hand to the accession of something, which is called "food" and is said to be "contrary" to flesh, but (b) on the other hand to the transformation of this food into the same form as that of flesh—as if, e. g., "moist" were to accede to "dry" and, having acceded, were to be transformed and to become "dry" [Dgc, 321b, f.].

In other words, what is growing is the particular thing, say bone or flesh; not the particles of matter involved, which matter in itself is never any particular thing.

An examination of these passages will not only clarify Aristotle's meaning with respect to this one problem, but at the same time it will help us to see what he meant by "form." It is true that in considering illustrations of coming-to-be from things which are constituted by art, such as a statue, the meaning of form seems often to be similar to three-dimensional outline. In a profounder sense, however, the form which the statue is to assume is something which preëxists in the mind of the artist. It is visible to him, and by the making of the statue it becomes visible to others. But with things constituted by nature, form as what one sees to be the essential nature of a thing is not outline, but characteristic activity. The difference may be illustrated by considering that in a statue it is always easy to distinguish between the marble as marble and the marble as statue. An operation may be performed to remove, say, a section of marble near the region roughly corresponding to the heart. If the operation is successfully performed, the statue of Hercules remains no less a statue of Hercules. But if Portia had not intervened to prevent this being tried on Antonio, the unlucky merchant would not have survived; that is, he would no longer engage in his characteristic activity of living. This is what would be meant by saying, in Aristotle's terms, that the operation would involve, together with a loss of flesh, a destruction of form without which the matter is no longer what it was, though most of it remain.

Every part of the body is thus involved in form, which is to say that the definition of a part is in terms of its function. This brings us back to Aristotle's definition of nature itself as "the distinctive form or quality of such things as have within themselves a principle of motion, such form or characteristic property not being separable from the things themselves, save conceptually" (Ph, 193b).

Now let us return to our organism growing in every part *qua* form but not *qua* matter. It becomes apparent that Aristotle is not escaping from a difficulty which exists when matter is talked about, by just talking about form instead. He has, rather, made it plain that the food by which the thing grows is not added as matter to the material constituents of the organism, but is changed into that which will function as the flesh or other organic part functions. Thus, while every part of the magnitude has grown, this has not involved the impossible situation of acceding bodies being in contact with every possible unit of matter. Just how the accession takes place is found to be aside from the point, which is that, as accession takes place, the form as a whole is necessarily changed. It is in observing how Aristotle uses the distinctions between matter and form in analyzing such problems that we can come closer to an understanding of his terms than is possible through examining a definition. The form of "form," so to speak, is what form does in its characteristic activity of explaining things!

In the coming-to-be of an organism, we have seen that it is not any matter which can be acted upon by the principle of movement to become a new thing, but matter which is so organized that it has determinate possibilities for receiving specific forms. On a different level of change, that of growth, we find a similar situation. Not *any* matter is that whereby an organism can increase, but matter, again, with determinate possibilities for being acted upon. For example, it is potentially flesh, if the increase of flesh is involved. Since it is flesh only potentially, actually it must be other than flesh, so that there is involved a coming-to-be of flesh. Aristotle distinguishes this transformation into flesh from coming-to-be, as it is usually considered, by saying that the food "has not been transformed into flesh alone by itself . . . on the contrary, it is the growing thing which has come-to-be flesh . . . *by* the food." That is, when the process is thought of in terms of coming-to-be, what is being considered is the growth of the part, not the change which takes place in the nature of the food. To characterize the latter as coming-to-be would mean that the food becomes a new thing; whereas it becomes, rather, part of something which already is. Therefore it "has not been transformed into flesh alone by itself," but it has been subjected to a change the obverse of which is the growth of the part involved (Dgc, 322a).

This modification of the food discloses a principle of growth as a highly significant aspect of the nature of an organism. By nature, a growing organism is characterized by the laying hold of food which is potentially that of which a given part is made and changing it into a constituent of that part (Dgc, 322a). We shall see presently that what is here described as "the active principle of growth" is so similar to what is explicitly attributed to psyche that we can be sure that Aristotle was not introducing this as anything distinct from the other factors he has described. Rather, the activity of growth is one of the characteristic activities of living, which is to say "ensouled," beings. This is a significant phase of Aristotle's theory, showing both the similarity and the difference between coming-to-be and growth. The more radical of the two changes takes place when a new thing comes into existence through material of determinate possibilities receiving the principle of movement. Increase is the less radical change, yet one which shows the dynamic character of things natural. For there is here the catching-up of the non-living into the living. It is similar to coming-to-be, in that material has become something different from what it was and, further, that this could not be *any* matter, but *appropriate* matter. It is dissimilar, in that the matter has not become something different *in itself*, but rather that some concrete thing has been changed *by* it.

Aristotle's emphasis on concrete things as the only true existences leads to a distinction between increase in size, abstractly considered, and enlargement of a particular part. He says that it is not quantity-in-general that comes-to-be in growth, just as it is not "animal," which is no specific form of animal, which comes-to-be in generation (Dgc, 322a). Rather, it is flesh or bone which comes-to-be in growth, as we have seen above. We were there considering the difference between coming-to-be, as usually considered, and growth, from the standpoint of the material involved. Here we can add that from the standpoint of the organism, coming-to-be, strictly speaking, is a term applied to the thing as a whole, while growth as a secondary type of coming-to-be is a term applied to parts.

### DIFFERENTIATION AND MATURATION OF THE PARTS

The most readily accessible method for the modern psychologist in attacking many of his problems is to study the behavior of animals in conditions varied under control. With the recent extensive investigations in the field of development from the embryonic stage, there have necessarily been many phases of experimentation which could be carried on only with subhuman forms. It is interesting to note that this method was used by Aristotle to settle difficult points regarding the generation and growth of organisms.

To illustrate, we may cite the problem of how human embryos are nourished in the uterus. Aristotle examined one hypothesis (1) by direct observation through dissection of other animals; (2) by examining the structures involved in the surrounding of embryos, to determine whether the conditions necessitated by the hypothesis existed; and (3) by citing facts which were unexplained by the hypothesis and which made it superfluous. It is worth while to give the account in Aristotle's words.

Those who say that children are nourished in the uterus by sucking some lump of flesh or other are mistaken. If so, the same would have been the case with other animals, but as it is we do not find this (and this can easily be observed by dissection). Secondly, all embryos alike, whether of creatures that fly or swim or walk, are surrounded by fine membranes separating them from the uterus and from the fluids which are formed in it; but neither in these themselves is there anything of the kind, nor is it possible for the embryo to take nourishment by means of any of them. Thirdly, it is plain that all creatures developed in eggs grow when separated from the uterus [Dga, 746a].

This use of the comparative method is one important characteristic of Aristotle's investigations of development.

A second characteristic is Aristotle's insistence upon the, search for specific, rather than abstract principles of explanation. For instance, he details an abstract proof to demonstrate the necessity of the mule's sterility—a proof which has the pleasant tang of sophistry. It ran as follows. The offspring of parents of the same species is of like species with the parents. When different species are sufficiently similar to cross, the offspring of these parents will be a hybrid, different in species from either of the parents. Let us say that the offspring of a member of species A and a member of species B is a member of Y, a third species. The condition therefore upon which a *y* can be produced is the union of an *a* and a *b*. But two members of the same species generate a member of the same species, so that two members of Y should produce a *y*. But, as we have seen, the condition to produce a *y* is ***not*** the union of two members of Y, but of an *a* and a *b*. Therefore, the members of Y must be sterile (Dga, 747b, f.).

As a logical argument showing why a mule, the offspring of horse and ass, must be sterile, the above seems to be perfectly sound. But Aristotle is not pleased with it, as it is

too general and empty. For all theories not based on the special principles involved are empty; they only appear to be connected with the facts without being so really. . . . Now the basis of this particular theory is not true, for many animals of different species are fertile with one another. . . . We shall be more likely to find the reason by considering the facts peculiar to the two kinds concerned, horse and ass [*ibid.*].

And then follows a description of the specific traits of these animals, which lead to the sterility of their hybrids. It is significant, however, that this rejection of rationalism as a method does not lead Aristotle to lose himself in mere description. Although he rejects the view that one can discover what exists by discovering the structure of discourse which goes on about it, still there are ultimate principles in nature which are involved in widely different ways in the infinite variety of things which are present to our observation. In the case under discussion he comes to conclusions in terms of fundamental principles, as hot and cold, with respect to the particular ways in which they are present in these species. Explanation must be in terms of principles, but of principles which are immediately involved, and *as* they are so involved, in the concrete thing which is under consideration.

There are two fundamental causes of differentiation. First, as we have seen repeatedly, the material which is contributed by the female is such that it has the power to receive specific forms. That this includes the detailed structure of the organism is made most explicit when Aristotle says that

. . . the parts are not differentiated . . . because like is naturally carried to like. . . . The real cause why each of them comes into being is that the secretion of the female is potentially such as the animal is naturally, and all the parts are potentially present in it, but none actually [Dga, 740b].

The second cause of the differentiation of the parts is the principle of movement received from the male, after the imparting of which "they develop in a chain one after another, as the wheels are moved one by another in the automatic machines" (Dga, 741b). The minimum implications of these passages are that the parts arise from the determinate potentialities of the material contributed by the female, and that they develop in serial order after receiving the principle of movement from the male. It must be kept in mind that when Aristotle says that something is potentially present, he means also, and by that very statement, that *actually* it is *not* there. The material, therefore, does not contain the parts, ready to grow, but is rather that out of which the parts can be actualized. With regard to the second principle, it is still more important to guard against reaching hasty conclusions concerning the nature of development from the analogy of the wheels in automatic machines. Just what Aristotle meant to convey will become clear when we later discuss the passages which describe in detail the order of development and why it is as it is.

In Aristotle's doctrine of development, heredity and final cause are viewed as two aspects of one fundamental fact: everything living comes from something like it, each part of which has a definite function. There is a consecutiveness of like organisms, so to speak, which can be thought of in terms of biological determination as heredity or described in speculative analysis as final cause. Empedocles had stated a doctrine excluding final cause, based on chance variations and natural selection through survival of the suitably formed. Aristotle rejected this view, in favor of an interpretation of nature which laid great stress on teleology. When we come to consider heredity in detail, we shall see that Aristotle recognized variations and sought to explain them. Here it is sufficient to note that the organism, as he viewed it, came to be what it was because (1) of the determining powers of the "creative seed" (2) which operated in accordance with final cause—the end of producing an organism with characteristics like the parents. Empedocles, said Aristotle,

> overlooked the fact that propagation implies a creative seed endowed with certain formative properties. Secondly, he neglected another fact, namely, that the parent animal pre-exists, not only in idea, but actually in time

(so that these formative properties must always be directly related to the parent, and not "the results of incidental occurrences during their development; for instance, that the backbone was divided as it is into vertebrae, because it happened to be broken owing to the contorted position of the foetus in the womb") (Dpa, 640a).

In turning to a detailed consideration of Aristotle's view of heredity, it will be sufficient with regard to the first point to restate in summary form two conclusions which we have noted. First, the characters which will eventuate in the completed organism are determined by the seed, which has formative properties (Dpa, 640a); and second, development is not merely addition: the semen is not only not an animal—it is not even blood and flesh, but the agent by which blood and flesh can be made (Dga, 723a).

We notice next a significant statement and one which must be analyzed carefully for its contribution to an understanding of Aristotle's doctrine of development: "It has been settled, then, in what sense the embryo and the semen have soul, and in what sense they have not; they have it potentially but not actually" (Dga, 737a). To say that semen has soul only potentially would not be hard to understand, but after the new organism has come to be, if the soul, which is to actualize the potentialities of the embryo is itself only potential, how is the actualization of the soul itself to be viewed?

Sometimes it appears that a writer has said something which has to be recast before it truly represents his position in general. But a safe principle on which to proceed is to interpret a passage in its own terms, without recourse to other suppositions, if such a restriction is at all practicable. To do otherwise leads a reader to the fallacy of harmonizing a writer's various statements with what the reader conceives the author to mean, rather than to the faithful educing of all the data necessary for an accurate interpretation of his doctrine.

In the case before us, we have an organism which has come-to-be. As such, we are dealing with post-generative phenomena, so far as the parents are concerned. Aristotle viewed birth, as it truly is, as an incident in the process of development, so that it is not relevant to say that after generation the embryo for some time is in contact with the mother's body. Even after birth, the organism is still not a perfect animal (Dga, 737b). We cannot appeal, therefore, to the begetter as the efficient cause—the cause must exist within the embryo itself.

We see, therefore, that we have what it is fair to designate as an "autarchic" organism. It has within it its own principles of development. Yet the soul, which we understand in terms of these internal principles of movement, is only potential and is actualized synchronously with the organism which it actualizes. On the surface this appears to be a paradoxical statement of the case. But let us take the statement as we find it, make explicit its implications, and then wait for evidence from the many converging sources to see if we have thereby arrived at a position which is true to Aristotle's doctrine of soul, more broadly considered.

One thing is plain to begin with: the soul, according to Aristotle, is not something which, in and of itself, acts. It is not something which acts upon the embryo. It is, however, something without which the embryo cannot act. But insofar as the embryo is potential animal, its soul is potential soul, the soul being actualized synchronously with the organism. Using the word in a sense analogous to its use in mathematics rather than in its biological sense, we see then that the soul is a function of the organism. When the organism is potential, the soul is potential; when the organism is fully actualized, the soul is fully actualized.

So far, we cannot make any statement relative to the priority of soul or organism. The organism would not be, were it not for the soul; but neither would the soul be, were it not for the organism. This complete mutuality is further expressed in *De anima* (414a):

> . . . the actuality of each thing is naturally inherent in its potentiality, that is in its own proper matter. From all this it is clear that the soul is the actuality and form of that which has the capacity of having a soul.

The exposition of this passage is difficult, but points toward saying that what we are really talking about, in all this problem of life, is an organism; and that soul, as what characterizes an organism, is a term which we use to express the difference between a dead body, which is subject only to external force, and a living body, which is moved also by forces whose principles are within it.

Returning to our original passage, we are in a position now to say that Aristotle, in holding that the embryo, which is only potentially an animal, has soul only potentially, is saying that the organism is our primary object and the true actor in development. Insofar as it lives it has life, which is to say, soul; as it lives more fully, it has fuller life, which is to say that as its potentialities are actualized, its soul is actualized; when it has reached full actuality, that actuality can again be expressed in terms of soul, which is "the first actuality of a natural body possessed of organs" (Da, 412b).

No technique was available to Aristotle for the investigation of the structure of what determined the likeness between parents and offspring, but the general conclusions to which he came on this point certainly point the way toward what has been accepted as established in recent times. Great stress was laid upon the importance of the blood of an organism and hence of the heart. The heart and the blood of the parent were of such character that the organs of that parent were made in a particular way. Then the semen, as the secretion of this blood, will be of such character that a similar heart and blood will result in the offspring. Therefore, since the heart and blood of the offspring are similar to the heart and blood of the parent, the organs which the blood of the offspring makes will resemble the organs which the blood of the parent made (Dga, 766b).

It should be observed that Aristotle does not accept the doctrine which had been offered, that the semen comes from every part of the parent body and that it goes to every part of the body directly. Without making too much of doctrinal consistency, it is nevertheless interesting to see how Aristotle's general dynamic view of things natural, enabling him to explain the coming-to-be of new things, enters all along the line to exclude naïve ideas of how the body could grow mechanically. The semen is not some product of each part of the body, which in turn will construct each part of the embryo. It is rather a product of the blood, which will give rise to similar blood (quite different from semen), which will give rise to parts (quite different from blood).

The dissimilarities which exist between parent and offspring are more intriguing, in a way, than the similarities. Whether or not one knows the mechanism involved in carrying hereditary characters, it seems reasonable that such likeness should exist. But why the wide variations which exist, and which seem to invalidate the view of predetermination? Aristotle's explanation was not as satisfactory as his account of resemblance. It could not be otherwise, for his great shortcoming was the failure to see the similarity between the male and the female contribution in generation, with the consequent possibilities of countless differences in combination. His view that the female contributes the material, the male the principle of movement, is inadequate to explain all the facts of parental resemblance, but when variations are considered the inadequacy is many times multiplied. It is significant, however, that he faced the problem and at least projected a hypothesis for its explanation.

Now that which is acted on escapes and is not mastered by the semen, either through deficiency of power in the concocting and moving agent or because what should be concocted and formed into distinct parts is too cold and in too great quantity. Thus the moving agent, mastering it in one part but not in another, makes the embryo in formation to be multiform [Dga, 768b].

While we have stated the inadequacy of this view, due to failure to recognize the combinations which are made between two lines of determination similar in function, it is exceedingly interesting to read this account, which does not sound totally unrelated to a discussion of the difference between dominant and recessive traits in terms of deficiency involved in the latter.

Aristotle's more definitely philosophical views as related to the problems of biology are involved in carrying through the discussion of variations to account for monsters. In these irregular organisms parts were frequently present which appeared to be parts of a different species. Aristotle believed, however, that this was deceiving to the eye and turned for explanation to the difference between individual and class characteristics.

Now the peculiar and individual has always more force in generation than the more general and wider characteristics. Coriscus is both a man and an animal, but his manhood is nearer to his individual existence than is his animal-hood. In generation both the individual and the class are operative, but the individual is the more so of the two, for this is the only true existence [Dga, 767b].

Therefore, if the activity of the semen fails to control the material contributed by the mother, that which would characterize an ordinary individual in the part concerned fails to be developed, and that which is a more general "animal" characteristic appears instead (Dga, 769b).

It will appear from our later discussion of Aristotle's view of necessity, as related to final cause, that the phenomena of variations in both their usual form and also in that of monsters are an illustration of things which come to pass by mechanical necessity, rather than in accordance with final cause.

The romantic question of where fancy is bred—in heart or in head—would not have detained Aristotle long. Even sex was determined by the quality of the heart. A first-rate heart produced a male. Factory-seconds turned out females. If this view was the result of antifeminism, at least the mischief was worked prior to this stage, for the conclusions follow quite logically from his biological premises. The argument is as follows: an organism is male or female according as it has, respectively, ability or inability to

> concoct the nourishment in its ultimate stage. . . . The cause of this capacity is in the first principle and in the part which contains the principle of natural heat [—the heart—Dga, 766a].

Therefore sex is determined by the heart, which we shall see is the organ formed first, because the heart will determine the sufficiency or insufficiency of vital heat to concoct the nourishment to the degree necessary to produce a male. However, this quality of the heart did not constitute sex; the organism is not male or female until this sufficiency or insufficiency of vital heat has resulted, at the proper stage, in the appearance of organs characteristic of male or female.

One question remains in our discussion of heredity. Why, among members of a given species, are there individual characteristics as well as those which distinguish the species as a whole? Aristotle did not discuss this in connection with variations from paternal pattern. It is, indeed, closely related, but is different in that in one case the question is why offspring should vary from parent, the offspring being generated by the parent; in the other case the question is why characters universally present in a species (which, however, generates nothing) have subcharacters, so to speak, which vary among individuals.

In the first of these questions, as we have seen, Aristotle found the solution in terms of the success or failure of the male principle to control the material contributed by the female. In the second question the solution is found in the presence or absence of final cause. We find here a doctrine which sets a limit to operations according to final cause and invokes necessity in its place. Final cause appears to be that which characterizes a given nature as a whole, rather than individuals in their varying traits. Or to begin our statement from the other end, individuals are generated and developed in accordance with final cause; but final cause is a factor only in the development of characters common to the class in which they belong. Their individual characteristics are to be determined not according to final cause but by necessity—which we shall have occasion to examine presently. "The eye for instance exists for a final cause, but it is not blue for a final cause unless this condition be characteristic of the kind of animal" (Dga, 778a).

What Aristotle is saying here is this: the natural phenomena of generation manifest, as we have had occasion to notice in our study, the consecutiveness of like organisms —every living being is generated by another of the *same kind*. This is the heart of the idea of final cause as applied to natural development: a process of generation is set in motion, the end of which is the production of a like organism. But let it be observed that there are not as many *kinds* of living beings as there are individuals. Therefore, if final cause is the term which we use to express the fact that every living creature is produced by another of the same kind, then to say that individuals are generated and developed in accordance with final cause is exactly the same as to say that each living being will have the characteristics common to its species. In thus distinguishing final cause as a factor in development, we can say that Aristotle distinguished it *from* something else (which he calls necessity), which expresses the further fact that each living being, in addition to characteristics common to the species, develops its own peculiarities. As he viewed this distinction, it could with accuracy be described as that which exists between functional and nonfunctional traits.

This distinction emphasizes the nonefficient character of final cause, which is sometimes forgotten when considering Aristotle's statement that it is first in generation. At the conclusion of the passage cited, there are words which can be misunderstood if taken by themselves, but which become quite clear in their meaning when considered in the preceding context:

> . . . when we are dealing with definite and ordered products of Nature, we must not say that each *is* of a certain quality be-

cause it *becomes* so, but rather that they *become* so and so because they *are* so and so, for the process of Becoming or development attends upon Being and is for the sake of Being, not vice versa [Dga, 778b].

The preceding context shows that "definite and ordered products of Nature" refers to individuals with respect to those characteristics which are common to their species. To that degree, final cause is a factor in development. But the variation of these characteristics among members of a species—or as we might say, the particular way in which these characters are present in an individual—is not ordered in accordance with final cause but by necessity.

This last topic, which we have considered under heredity, since it deals with the determination of characters in physiological terms (involved in necessity), also introduces us to the study of final cause. Aristotle worked this principle to the limit, and we shall do well to understand his specific meaning as closely as we can.

In the quotation which opened this study, we heard Aristotle speaking of the lowly animals which, having "no graces to charm the sense" yet disclose "to intellectual perception the artistic spirit that designed them" and

give immense pleasure to all who can trace links of causation, and are inclined to philosophy. . . . Absence of haphazard and conduciveness of everything to an end are to be found in Nature's works in the highest degree, and the resultant end of her generations and combinations is a form of the beautiful [Dpa, 645a].

This is for Aristotle a rare, poetical passage. It discloses his thinking at a point where scientific interest blends with the attitude of reverence—where the fact of design which he finds in the universe around him leads him to express that fact in figurative and esthetic terms.

Assuming a little of this poetic liberty, let us say that a key principle in Aristotle's view of design was elegance—more prosaically, economy. He was justified in pushing the inquiry relative to the end of each thing which he examined, "For nature never makes anything that is superfluous" (Dpa, 691b). This is exactly the reverse of the views of some modern scientists, according to whom everything comes to be, without purpose of any kind being involved. This results in the prodigal production of the superfluous, so that Aristotle's key principle of economy is completely reversed.

We have had occasion to observe that final cause is the first among the causes of an organism's generation.

> The causes concerned in the generation of the works of nature are, as we see, more than one. There is the final cause and there is the motor cause. . . . Plainly, however, that cause is the first which we call the final one. For this is the Reason [λόγος], and the Reason forms the starting-point, alike in the works of art and in the works of nature [Dpa, 639b].

Aristotle says plainly here, first, that when an organism is generated, regardless of the mechanical sequence which is involved, the process cannot be understood aside from the goal toward which it moves. In other words, he says that the mechanics are as they are because they are the particular mechanics which are involved in such an organism; rather than that the organism is as it is because such mechanics exist. Second, he makes it plain that this final cause doesn't *do* anything. It is the starting point of an adequate understanding or explanation; to initiate a natural process, on the other hand, a "motor cause" must act on appropriate material.

We have seen that there is often an identity between the final and formal causes: ". . . for the essential nature of a thing and the purpose for which it is produced are often identical" (Ph, 198a). Since "this applies universally to all things that cause motion and are themselves moved" (*ibid.*), final cause is most closely involved in that which constitutes an organism what it is. In an extended discussion of why the inquirer into nature must concern himself about the soul, he speaks of

> nature as essence including both the motor cause and the final cause. Now it is in the latter of these two senses that either the whole soul or some part of it constitutes the nature of an animal [Dpa, 641a].

A dead body is not a man, because that which constitutes it a man is not present (Dpa, 640b).

> For just as human creations are the products of art, so living objects are manifestly the products of an analogous cause or principle, not external but internal, derived like the hot and the cold from the environing universe. . . . It is evident that there must be a something or other really existing, corresponding to what we call by the name of Nature [Dpa, 641b].

These statements show not only that living objects are produced in accordance with final cause; this final cause is internal to the organism itself. Yet it is derived from the environing universe, which appears to be Nature and which appears to be spoken of in this connection as an existent thing. At all events, it is a fair representation of Aristotle's views to say that this factor of final cause characterizes things natural. Organisms are members of this great kingdom and, as such, have this factor within themselves. It is derived from the universe, in that the organism in which it resides is a part of a kingdom of things which are thus characterized; and it is internal because that is the way it is effective with respect to those things.

In the discussion of generation we saw how Aristotle considered it necessary for the natural philosopher to distinguish the four causes. Yet often, and so far as the things with which we are now exclusively interested are concerned always, three of these causes coincide: the final, formal, and efficient (Ph, 198a). It was evident, too, that psyche for Aristotle was what functioned as these three causes. We are now concerned with psyche functioning as final cause.

One passage quoted in Chapter I states the case quite fully. Each part of the body is for some partial end. The whole body is designed for a complete type of activity. It is then explicitly stated that "the body too must somehow or other be made for the soul, and each part of it for some subordinate function, to which it is adapted" (Dpa, 645b).

The great part of *De partibus animalium* is devoted to the work of showing the "partial ends" of the various structures of organisms. We shall consider only a few examples of his treatment, selecting those which illustrate, in man, the functioning of psyche as final cause.

The character of man's speech is one thing which most widely distinguishes him from other animals. It is to be expected, therefore, that Aristotle would discuss the organs requisite for this activity. Especially noteworthy is his discussion of the overlapping of functions to be found involved in a single structure.

For just as nature has made man's tongue unlike that of other animals, and, in accordance with what I have said is her not uncommon practice, has used it for two distinct operations, namely for the perception of savours and for speech, so also has she acted with regard to the lips, and made them serve both for speech and for the protection of the teeth. For vocal speech consists of combinations of the letters, and most of these it would be impossible to pronounce, were the lips not moist, nor the tongue such as it is [Dpa, 659b, f.].

He emphasizes the unique suitability of man's tongue for speech (*ibid.*). The above quotation shows how the lips have the double function of facilitating speech and protecting the teeth, but later (Dpa, 661b) we see, too, that "In man . . . the number and the character even of these sharp teeth have been mainly determined by the requirements of speech."

The adaptability of man's hand for the ends of intelligence has shared attention with the organs of speech. Just how the hand is related to intelligence is still a subject of interest, and Aristotle and Anaxagoras in ancient times held divergent views on this modern problem.

Now it is the opinion of Anaxagoras that the possession of these hands is the cause of man being of all animals the most intelligent. But it is more rational to suppose that his endowment with hands is the consequence rather than the cause of his superior intelligence. For the hands are instruments or organs, and the invariable plan of nature in distributing the organs is to give each to such animal as can make use of it; nature acting in this matter as any prudent man would do [Dpa, 687a].

Anaxagoras, that is, begins with the hand and uses it to understand why man is the most intelligent of animals, while Aristotle starts with man's superior intelligence and finds that it involves the use of the remarkably adaptable hand, as one of a complex system of parts which the organism as a whole "necessitates"—in the sense which we shall presently describe.

Aristotle applies this reasoning to the erect posture of man, but in a way which has less meaning for us.

> For of all animals man alone stands erect, in accordance with his godlike nature and essence. For it is the function of the godlike to think and to be wise; and no easy task were this under the burden of a heavy body, pressing down from above and obstructing by its weight the motions of the intellect and of the general sense [Dpa, 686a].

This way of stating the case is foreign to our view of "the motions of the intellect and of the general sense," but we can agree entirely that an erect posture is essential to the functioning of the human organism. We could, indeed, connect the matter of posture with the use of the hand, which we have seen to be so significant; it is evident that the hand could not function as it does were not man's posture erect.

It may be seen from these quotations that Aristotle believed in the close correlation of man's distinct superiority in psyche over the other animals with his corresponding superiority of requisite organs. Evidently there were those in his day, as there are now, who think that man, considered as an animal, is very inferior, forgetting the relationship which exists between his superior mentality and certain unique structures. "Much in error, then, are they who say that the construction of man is not only faulty, but inferior to that of all other animals" (Dpa, 687a).

Having discussed heredity and final cause as different

aspects of the cause of differentiation, we now turn to consider necessity. It fairly represents Aristotle's view to say that the activity of differentiation which may be thought of as due to heredity on the one hand and to final cause on the other, takes place in accordance with necessity. We have already considered mechanical necessity as involved in the development of traits which are not common to a species, such as blueness of eye. In that case, final cause was not involved; but we shall now see that development is in accordance with necessity of a different kind, even when final cause is a determining factor.

In *Metaphysica* (1015a, b) Aristotle defines a simple sense of "necessary" as meaning that which cannot be otherwise. All other senses of the term are derived from this one. For example, "compulsory necessity" describes that which cannot be otherwise because impulse or purpose is restrained. The two senses in which things are said to occur by necessity, with which we are here concerned, are the mechanical and the teleological. The former type of activity springs from the nature of material as affected by an efficient cause only (Ph, 200a), as we have seen in the instance of eye color where one color is not common to the members of the species. It is clear from the argument of *Physica,* Book II, chapters iv–vi, that one kind of "chance" and "mechanical necessity" deseribe the same natural phenomena. For every event has a cause—but chance events are produced "incidentally" by factors otherwise directed; they are thus produced by necessity rather than in accordance with final cause.

The teleological type of activity which nevertheless occurs by necessity (Ph, Book II, chap. ix; Dpa, 640ff.) is controlled by the end to be achieved. For in the achieving of ends there are conditions involved which are "necessary." A house is not necessitated by stones, bricks, timber, and the forces which naturally affect these materials—that would be mechanical necessity. But if a house is to exist, then materials must be used—that is the teleological, or hypothetical necessity. An illustration of Aristotle's use of necessity in the latter sense is found in his discussion of homogeneous and heterogeneous parts.

> So far, then, as has yet been stated, the relations between these two orders of parts are determined by a final cause. We have, however, to inquire whether necessity may not also have a share in the matter; and it must be admitted that these mutual relations could not from the very beginning have possibly been other than they are [Dpa, 646b].

The foregoing illustrates the "necessary" relations which exist between different parts. A related principle is that physiological resources determine the order of development of parts. The eyes, for instance, "are perfected late because of the amount of concoction required by the brain, and last of all the parts because the motion must be very strong before it can affect parts so far from the first principle of motion and so cold" (Dga, 744b).

This principle itself, however, does not stand alone, for the physiological resources themselves are found to be available for parts in an order of priority according to function. "Those [parts] most honourable and participating in the sovereign principle" are formed out of the best of the nutriment. The parts which exist because they are necessary for the functioning of those which are thus primary are formed out of inferior nutriment and from the residues of the best. This is also true of the embryo, in which the best material is used to form the flesh and the sense organs; from the residues come the bones, sinews, hair, nails, and hoofs. Accordingly, these latter assume their form last, having to wait upon the availability of material (Dga, 744b). This explains why the body of man differs so much from other animals in natural coverings and weapons. "It is because such parts are formed from a residue that man is the most naked in body of all animals and has the smallest nails in proportion to his size; he has the least amount of earthy residue, but that part of the blood which is not concocted is the residue, and the earthy part in the bodies of all animals is the least concocted" (Dga, 745b).

Finally, the relationship of necessity is apparent in the synchronous appearance of functions and structures. "Hence each region comes into being along with the secretions and the faculties, as e. g. the faculty of sight is not perfected without the eye, nor the eye without the faculty of sight" (Dga, 766a). Platt says that Aristotle is not always consistent on this point, but as thus stated it sums up well the conception of hypothetical necessity.

Closely related to the function of necessity in development is the fact that growth involves a comprehensive sequence of activity. Aristotle distinguishes three degrees of composition. First is the primary composition out of the elements. Next come the homogeneous structures, such as bones and flesh, which are composed of the "primary substances" of the foregoing degree. In the final stage the heterogeneous parts are composed from the homogeneous

(Dpa, 646a). This passage has within it the main outline of Aristotle's description of development. It shows, first of all, the coming-to-be of organic substance through the use of simple physical elements, as we have discussed above in connection with nutrition. Given organic substance, we have the development first of relatively undifferentiated and then of relatively differentiated structures.

Aristotle's distinction between the order of development and the order of logical existence is justly famous, helping to explain, as it does, Aristotle's view of final cause.

> Now the order of actual development and the order of logical existence are always the inverse of each other. For that which is posterior in the order of development is antecedent in the order of nature, and that is genetically last which in nature is first. . . . In order of time, then, the material and the generative process must necessarily be anterior to the being that is generated; but in logical order the definitive character and form of each being precedes the material [Dpa, 646a, b].

Taken in connection with our former discussion, this paragraph reëmphasizes the fact that there exists, antecedently to the development of a specific organism, the form of that organism considered as the general form of the species as a whole. That is what might be called the "logical" view of the facts. But when the time factor is introduced, logical order gives way to the order of development, and the general form of the species as a whole gives way to the form of the individual. Here the order is reversed, and we have the full potentialities of form actualized at the end of a process of development. And since this actualized form is the organism in its most differentiated form, we may further say that the development of an organism follows the general pattern of progress from undifferentiated mass to differentiated structure.

Yet there is a sense in which the new form as a whole is in the embryo from the beginning: namely, it has the determinate potentiality of becoming a fully matured organism of the same species, such as material of a different kind does not have. The parts of animals develop successively, and Aristotle raises the question as to whether a part comes into existence because of the one which preceded it or whether it merely comes into being *after* the other part. On the ground that the former view would mean that "the form and character of the later organ would have to exist in the earlier" (Dga, 734a), it is rejected. One organ comes into being after another, but not by the agency of the former. This extended passage makes it very clear that, regardless of the role played by necessity in the interaction of the embryo and its environment, the primary factor in the process of the issuing of development as it does is the determinate potentiality of the organism which characterizes it from the beginning.

We have seen, however, that this does not imply any approach to the theory of preformation, and the close of the passage cited above reëmphasizes this point: "Yet again, if the whole animal or plant is formed from [by] semen or seed, it is impossible that any part of it should exist ready made in the semen or seed, whether the part be able to make the other parts or no."

In achieving this final form there are certain relationships of priority which are observed. Three things are distinguished in this connection: the end, for the sake of which the organs exist; the "principle of movement and of generation," which makes the end possible; and the instruments of the end. The first of these is prior in the logical view we have discussed, but in actual development we have, of course, something quite different. Yet this different order of development is not stated exactly as we would expect on the basis of reversing the logical order, but is complicated to do justice to what seemed to be the observed facts. "Accordingly, there must first exist some part in which is the principle of movement . . . ; next after this the whole and the end; thirdly and lastly, the organic parts serving these for certain uses" (Dga, 742a). The second of these stages refers to the upper half of the body, whose structure is for the sake of the end of the organism as a whole, as distinct from the lower half, whose structure is for the use of the upper.

When this order of priority is described more specifically, the heart occupies a place of determining significance. "For the definitive characteristic of an animal is the possession of sensation; and the first sensory part is that which first has blood; that is to say is the heart, which is the source of blood and the first of the parts to contain it" (Dpa, 666a, b). In another passage the heart is again given primacy, not this time because of its relation to sensation, but because it contains the principle of increase. A living thing "is produced, then, by something else of the same name, as e. g. man is produced by man, but it is increased by means of itself" (Dga, 735a). In animals which have a heart, the heart is the part from which arises the principle of movement. This principle embraces more than increase, being involved in the process of differentiation. In a sense, all the organs exist together in the embryo potentially. But the heart is nearest actualization and is a determining factor in the actualization of the rest.

> Therefore the heart is first differentiated in actuality. . . . It must have a first principle from which comes the ordering of the body at a later stage also. . . . When each of the parts is separating from the rest, it is necessary that this principle should exist first from which comes growth and movement to the other parts [Dga, 740a].

In this passage the central place accorded the heart as the principle or origin is on the basis of the organism's need of nourishment, which exists of course from the first. But this view is further confirmed by the history of the heart—

> for life fails in the heart last of all, and it happens in all cases that what comes into being last fails first, and the first last, Nature running a double course, so to say, and turning back to the point from whence she started. For the process of becoming is from the non-existent to the existent, and that of perishing is back again from the existent to the non-existent [Dga, 741b].

With regard to organs other than the heart, we shall only point out certain leading principles. In the description of the three degrees of composition, we saw how the final stage was the composition of the heterogeneous parts out of the homogeneous. This is an instance of the earlier stages taking place for the sake of the end result.

> Animals, then, are composed of homogeneous parts, and are also composed of heterogeneous parts. The former, however, exist for the sake of the latter [Dpa, 646b].

The stages through which an organism passes in its development through embryonic and to mature form have been the subject of various kinds of explanation. Aristotle found the explanation in terms of the passage from general characters to particular. We have already seen that soul is actualized synchronously with the organism, as, indeed, a characteristic of the organism. This is consistently stated in connection with the phenomena before us—of development from the general to the particular. There first exists in the embryo the nutritive soul; then the sensitive soul; finally, the soul which characterizes the particular animal.

For e. g. an animal does not become at the same time an animal and a man or a horse or any particular animal. For the end is developed last, and the peculiar character of the species is the end of the generation in each individual [Dga, 736b].

The internal parts are developed before the external. The larger ones are visible before the smaller, "even if some of them do not come into being before them" (Dga, 741b).

The preceding description has dealt almost exclusively with the order of development of the different parts. There is a further problem—the development of the particular part itself. Aristotle makes it plain that here, too, the progress is, in general, from mass to differentiated form. The outlines of the parts first appear, and later the particular characteristics, such as color and relative hardness. He likens this to an artist sketching the outlines of an animal and then filling in the detail (Dga, 743b).

The one problem of development which appears to baffle Aristotle completely is "When and how and whence is a share in reason [νοῦς] acquired by those animals that participate in this principle" (Dga, 736b). We recall the general doctrine that soul and organism are actualized from their potentialities concurrently. But in the case of reason we have no corresponding bodily "part." No other activity of the organism is without such part or parts on which it depends, so "It remains, then, for the reason [νοῦς] alone so to enter [from outside] and alone be divine, for no bodily activity has any connexion [anything common] with the activity of reason" (Dga, 736b). This doctrine, which is apparently so inconsistent with the general pattern of Aristotle's thought, has been a standing problem through centuries of Aristotelian interpretation. Its significance cannot be seen in the biological context in which it is given. A clue, however, may be found in *De anima* (429a), where Aristotle approves the doctrine that the thinking faculty of the soul (the νοῦς of the passage quoted above) is the place of forms. It has no actual existence except when it thinks. When it does think, or in the words of our passage, when there is an "activity of reason," it is occupied with forms. Forms of what? The answer is found to include the scope of the universe. This includes, of course, the organism itself. But the typical direction of Greek thought was outward to the world about, rather than inward, and it is not inconceivable that when Aristotle speaks of the principle of νοῦς as entering from without he had just this in mind—that νοῦς actual was occupied with forms, and the forms were of things outside. The detailed consideration of this view of the mind must be left for the discussion of Chapter IV, but here it is helpful to point out that while Aristotle unexpectedly removes the actualization of νοῦς from the actualization of the body, he does not thereby remove it from control. To use a figurative paradox: νοῦς was strictly limited —and the sky was the limit!

The immense importance attached today to glands and their influence on physical and mental characters is foreshadowed in Aristotle's view that some of the specific parts of an animal are themselves principles. He had no knowledge of hormones or their means of operation, but he observed the kind of phenomena which are assigned to them today. What characterizes such a part is that a change in it affects the entire organism, instead of only the area concerned. He illustrates this by the case of eunuchs, who, being mutilated in but one part, change so much from their normal appearance that they become in form much like females. "The reason of this is that some of the parts are principles, and when a principle is moved or affected needs must many of the parts that go along with it change with it" (Dga, 766a).

Our last consideration in the general problem of growth concerns efficiency. It is quite clear what Aristotle means by the material, formal, and final causes in the growth of an organism. We have seen, too, that in the type of phenomena which we are considering the formal, final, and efficient causes coincide, psyche functioning as each one. Just how this is worked out in the case of the efficient cause is harder to understand than in the case of the other two. Efficiency in development is one of the fields most inaccessible to investigation. With the improved methods of modern science, very little is yet known about it, and, with the complete absence of scientific chemistry in Aristotle's time, it is not surprising that his accounts of efficient cause in natural phenomena were less significant than those of the other causes. Concerning the problem before us, Aristotle puts the matter thus:

But how is each part formed? We must answer this by starting in the first instance from the principle that, in all products of Nature or art, a thing is made by something actually existing out of that which is potentially such as the finished product. Now the semen is of such a nature, and has in it such a principle of motion, that when the motion is ceasing each of the parts comes into being, and that as a part having life or soul . . . when we come to the principle in virtue of which flesh is flesh and bone is bone, . . . what makes them is the movement set up by the male parent, who is in actuality what that out of which the offspring is made is in potentiality [Dga, 734b].

From this passage we may gather these conclusions: first, whatever makes the parts is an actuality, not a potentiality; second, the only actuality involved is, not the semen, but the male parent, since the semen only potentially contains the soul which is requisite to constitute even flesh or bone what it is; third, Aristotle therefore, in treating the phenomena of growth, must have thought of it as a continuing result of the generative act. This is substantiated by the words, "Now the semen is of such a nature, and has in it such a principle of motion, that when the motion is ceasing each of the parts comes into being, and that as a part having life or soul" (*ibid.*). This further justifies our treatment of generation and growth as processes which, while distinguishable and having unique characteristics, are yet different aspects of one fundamental activity.

*Chapter Three*

# THE INITIATION AND CONTROL OF BEHAVIOR

WHAT CONSTITUTES the subject matter of psychology is still a subject of controversy. It is thought by some that emphasis on behavior obscures the primary meaning of the term, which indicates by its derivation that it concerns the soul. In Aristotle's psychology, however, we have the close union of physiology, behavior, and soul. The union is expressed in his definition of the soul as "the first actuality of a natural body possessed of organs" (Da, 412b). This first actuality is the potentiality of action—of the action of the organs as they are parts of an organism. Psychology in Aristotle's terms, therefore, must primarily concern behavior, since the soul is defined in functional terms. This behavior involves various factors. Foremost among them is appetence (ὄρεξις), which may be considered in its potentiality as the power of the organism to be stimulated to desire by an object in the environment, or in its actuality as the desiring or craving of the organism for some satisfaction to be found in or through activity. How is appetence aroused? The environment has certain stimulating effects which are produced in the organism by means of a second factor—its sensing. Finally, in the rational soul of man we have thought, which is a controlling factor in human behavior; and, in those animals which do not have the power of reason, imagination (φαντασία), as a lower form of "mental" process, is conceded as contributing to the production of movement. But all these are aspects of a total type of activity which a given kind of organism displays. Necessarily psychology must also concern itself with the physiological foundations of these types of behavior, since functions are functions of parts.

Our first interest will be the investigation of the way in which the activity of the organism is initiated, directed, and controlled. This inquiry can well be begun on the lower plane of animal life, for the soul is the principle of all living beings (Da, 402a). If we consider first what it is that happens when an "irrational animal" is moved to action, we can then see with profit how this is modified by the interacting processes of thinking on higher levels of life.

## MIND AND APPETENCE DISTINGUISHED

Aristotle accepted the views of his predecessors that two things distinguished that which has soul (excluding plants) from that which has not: movement and sensibility (Da, 403b). These are powers which belong to all animals, and the general analysis, as we shall see it presently, shows them to be interdependent. Movement is not something which arises spontaneously, but is a function of the environment and the condition of the organism, these two factors being so related by nature that certain aspects of the environment have stimulating effects on certain determinate capacities for action of the organism. Sensation is thus basically necessary for the production of movement, since it is through the sensing of the organism that the environment acts upon it.

From time to time we have noticed Aristotle's reference to a part or parts of the soul, and, before proceeding with a discussion which will make more specific use of such expressions, it is well to make sure of Aristotle's point of view regarding this division. In the opening pages of *De anima* (402b) the following questions are raised as pertinent to his inquiry: does the soul have parts or not and, if it has parts, should the soul as a whole be examined first, or the several parts? As the treatment proceeds, it becomes clear that when Aristotle refers to parts of the soul he is talking about functions which can be distinguished for purposes of discussion, and not parts which have separate existence, as a leg is separate from an arm or even from a foot. This is made clear in the last part of the work (432a, b), where he says that the various ways in which the soul can be divided seem to be indefinite in number. The particular division which is made seems to be determined by the purpose of the one who is talking, so that it may be rational, passionate, appetitive; or rational, irrational; or nutritive, sensitive, imaginative; and into none of these divisions does appetite fit neatly, as it is found in connection with different functions of the soul. From all this it is clear that when Aristotle refers to parts of the soul, he is referring to functions which can be separated for purposes of discussion.

Aristotle's analysis of the parts of the soul in reference to movement shows how the basic factor is common to all animals. The nutritive part of the soul, indeed, cannot be responsible for movement, since the latter is directed to a goal, implying imagination and appetence. It cannot be the sensitive part alone, or the sensitive soul would imply the presence of organs of locomotion, even in animals which are wholly stationary, since functions are necessarily functions of parts. From these faculties which are common to living things below the level of human life, Aristotle turns to the power which distinguishes man and says that movement is not due to the mind in its capacity of speculative thought, which does not deal with matters of action. Except under compulsion, one does not move except to pursue or avoid something, and hence desire is a necessary factor in producing movement. This is further shown to be the case by the fact that "appetite produces movement contrary to calculation," but even when one moves according to calculation, the movement is also in accordance with intention or purpose, which is a form of appetence (Da, 432b, f.). The initiation of activity, then, is not due to the functions of the soul, which are present below the level of animal life, nor to those which are present only in man; it is due to something which distinguishes animals as such.

## APPETENCE

This prime factor in causing movement—appetence—is described in terms of interaction between the organism and its environment. This relationship is made clear in both *De anima* (433b) and *De motu animalium* (700b–

703a). Here Aristotle deals with the way in which an environmental object, which itself is unmoved, sets the organism in motion. The total moving cause is immediately broken up into stimulus and response (response being considered in the wide sense of any actualization of a potentiality of the organism by stimulation of the environment), the stimulus-response relationship between the environment and the organism being in accordance with the nature of the organism, which nature itself may be defined in terms of determinate capacities to respond to environmental factors. The analysis is in three terms: "first the moving cause, secondly the means by which it produces movement, and thirdly the thing moved" (Da, 433b). The practical good, which is the end to which appetence is directed, is the unmoved moving cause. This produces the activity of appetence in the organism, which, related as it is to the potentialities of the organism, becomes a mover of a second order: a moved mover. That is, the activity of appetence is *the manner in which* the external cause, being unaffected itself (in this capacity) produces movement. This appetence is a bodily function and, considered as such (that is, as the craving only), it is something actual. In another sense, however, it is potential movement, so that "the movement is a form of appetence actualized" (Da, 433b).

In explaining why it is that bodily pleasures have the greatest appeal to some, Aristotle states as one reason that "many are so constituted that a neutral state of feeling is to them positively painful." This, in turn, rests upon the fact that "a state of strain is the normal condition of an animal organism, as physiology testifies; it tells us that sight and hearing are in fact painful, but we have got used to them in course of time—such is the theory" (EN, 1154b). This normal state of strain can be looked upon as appetence in its most general aspect, or again as that which puts or keeps the body in a state prepared for the activity of appetence.

Appetence is thus the intermediate factor between the external, unmoved end, or goal, and the moved organism. If the organism were activated by pure speculation, it would be something apart from the world of natural things around it—judging them, acting upon them, without being stimulated by them or acted upon by them. The alternative is not a piece of machinery whose movement can be explained in terms of mechanics, but an autarchic organism; with the further qualification that the ἀρχαί of the organism, at every point, concern the environing world.

## THE PRACTICAL MIND

This is not to say that desire operates simply. In man movement in space is produced by mind and desire working together, in which connection imagination, which many times controls action contrary to knowledge, is grudgingly thought of as a kind of thinking process. This is, indeed, the only kind of mental factor which contributes to producing movement in subhuman animals (Da, 433a). That much is necessary, for it enters into the total situation of the organism's being stimulated by the environment by means of sensation. In man, appetence remains the basic factor, but the total cause of movement becomes more complex, in a way which Aristotle explains by analyzing the parts or functions of the soul. The irrational part is divided into two functions: the first, which is vegetative, causes nutrition and growth, and exists even in embryos. The second is appetitive and in itself is irrational, as is the first; yet it is susceptible to rational control and hence can be said to participate in reason (EN, 1102b, f.). The rational part of the soul likewise may be divided into two functions, one of which speculates about those things whose principles are invariable, and the other of which calculates or deliberates about things which vary (EN, 1139a).

The speculative mind is not concerned with ends, but with science for science's sake, so to speak. What Aristotle calls the "practical mind," however, is engaged with the means of reaching the end to which appetence is directed. This end is the starting point of the practical mind, which reasons its way back to the step which will be taken first in the course of action designed to reach the objective (Da, 433a).

The analysis of this practical mind in *De anima* (433a) is almost identical with a passage in *De motu animalium* (700b). The thing which is the primary cause of movement is not just any object of intellect, but such an object as constitutes a practical end, which is to say, an object to which appetence is directed. Or, instead of being the end itself, it may be something necessary to the end. In either case the real or supposed good, which is the practical end, is identified as the object of desire and the beginning of the practical mind.

It is seen from this definition that the thoroughgoing intimacy between the organism and its environmental context is the controlling principle of Aristotle's analysis of this aspect of mind. Evidently the practical mind, as also the speculative mind, actually exists only when it is acting. The thing craved for is the origin, beginning, or principle of this mind in its actual existence and is therefore the ultimate "single moving cause." This is entirely analogous to Aristotle's view that mind is the place of forms, potentially existing. The forms are also the forms of the objects of thought. Similarly, the object of appetence is not something apart from the practical mind, but is the very ἀρχή of that mind.

In simplest terms, the action of the practical mind may be schematized as syllogistic reasoning. This is expressed in summary form in *De anima* (434a) and more fully in *De motu animalium* (701a); it is also used in discussing the effect of knowledge on conduct (EN, 1147a). Two different kinds of syllogism are offered in illustration, the conclusion in each case necessarily being an action. In one case there is argument from a universal, which relates to an action (such as "a man in such a position should act in such a way" [Da, 434a]), and a particular, which places the reasoner within the sphere of the universal. The conclusion, which is an action, follows unless there is something which hinders; from the total discussion it may be inferred that the hindrance may be either external or internal. In the other case (Dma, 701a) the argument is of different form. Here the major premise is the expression of desire: "I want to drink"; the minor premise is the identification by imagination, perception, or thinking, of some object in the environment which will satisfy the desire. Again the conclusion is an action.

The context of this discussion shows that Aristotle is

talking in schematic terms. He is stating the form of the practical mind which is implicit in its whole procedure, rather than describing a temporal process. In the syllogism of the second type, the major premise which begins the argument is an expression of desire, and the minor premise identifies the object. Actually, Aristotle says immediately following the description of this argument, that "desire is the last or immediate cause of movement," and he later restates that desire is prepared by imagination, which in turn depends on either conception or sense-perception. The fundamental point he is driving at here is the definition of the practical mind as a function of the body; just as in saying that the object desired is the starting point or principle of the practical mind, he emphasized its intimacy with the environment. The organism is so related to its environment that an external object puts into operation the process which Aristotle calls the practical mind. But this practical mind itself is the function of a body possessed of organs, so that its conclusions necessarily involve the activity of the appropriate organs. Then why does the conclusion—an action—not always follow? It does, except when externally hindered, which removes the failure at once from need of explanation; or when it is internally hindered by other actions of the practical mind—the phenomenon of conflict so important in all modern psychology. We shall examine Aristotle's analysis of conflict in some detail at a later point of our discussion.

This analysis shows that ideomotor activity is the rule, if nothing hinders; and that if the hindrance is from within, the rule is complicated rather than abrogated. But Aristotle's distinction of the practical from the speculative mind must be carefully kept before us in considering this doctrine. It is not cool contemplation which fires one to action; it is the operation of the practical mind, which has to do with ends to be achieved, and these are the particular ends to which appetence is directed. Appetence, then, is entirely fundamental in what still may be termed "ideo-motor activity."

As we have seen by our analysis thus far, this interaction between the organism and its environment is manifested in the phenomena of motivation equally in what may be termed their mental and their appetitive aspects. The practical mind, which is the reasoning function as it concerns itself with goals to be achieved, has its beginning or principle in the end to be sought—which at the same time is the end to which appetence is directed. Its reasoning covers the intermediate steps necessary to reach the goal, and hence its last step is identical with the movement of the organism. Appetence, likewise, is put into activity by the end to be achieved and it, being fully actualized, is the beginning of the organism's movement. Obviously we have before us, in the practical mind and in appetence, not two separate things but two different ways in which one organism is acted upon by its stimulating environment. It is stimulated to crave and, having a mind whose purpose is to be of service (or rather having the potentiality of doing useful thinking), it is simultaneously stimulated to seek means appropriate to satisfy desire. The means being found, the end of the practical mind is reached in the movement which is also the actualization of the appetite.

## APPETENCE AND THE FOUR CAUSES

In the analysis of activity which goes on "by nature," Aristotle consistently distinguishes the four causes and believes that they comprehend everything which legitimately can be considered as a causal factor. We are now faced with a particular situation, namely, the activity of a living being. In describing it, we have talked in terms of mind and appetence and have not mentioned the four causes at all. The interesting question arises, is the motivating power of appetence something which can be analyzed in terms of the four causes, or does Aristotle here deal with causation of a completely different order?

In the generation of an organism, we have seen that "parts" and "functions" are comprehensive terms under which may be subsumed the conditions of development and experience. The body as a whole constitutes the material of an organism; and its development is involved in the actualization of the form, which is the function of the body considered as a whole, since function involves structure. But this material basis of the organism's activity is not one uniform mass. It is an integration of a multitude of parts—or we may prefer to say that a multitude of integrated parts have been differentiated in the course of development. Flesh, bone, and heterogeneous parts can be distinguished; and each of these, in turn, comprises the four elements.

What the analysis into parts is for the body of an organism, the analysis of activity is for the form. The form is not one simple thing, just as the body is not. Nor is it one *kind* of thing, just as the body comprises parts which are wholly different in their structure. Psychology proper, so to speak, consists therefore in the analysis of behavior into its constituents; and since in analyzing behavior one is dealing with behavior from first to last, and since this behavior is the form, whatever that behavior is found to involve cannot be otherwise than a constituent of the organism's form.

Not leaving the question with this abstract answer, however, we shall more specifically relate the description of appetence to that of form. The behavior motivated by appetence will always be within the total pattern of behavior which characterizes the species as a whole—its form. There is an end to be achieved which is the final cause of the consequent activity—an end suggested by and involved in the environing world. Appetence is thus not a mere restlessness of the organism, but is a craving related to something in the external world. To satisfy this craving there must therefore be activity of a kind appropriate to changing the relationship between this external object and the organism, in a way satisfactory to the latter. This is accomplished by an efficient cause, appetence, which we have found to be potential activity, the actualization of which is the movement of the organism.

Appetence, therefore, is a cause of overt activity, which can be stated perfectly well in the familiar terms of formal, final, and efficient cause. It is the determinate kind of activity which characterizes the organism in any particular situation and which is thus its form. It is not an activity which springs only from within, or which is imposed from without; it is an activity which reveals the intimacy between an organism and its environment. The form of the organism is such that it cannot be explained, except in terms of the organism's own potentialities to be stimulated in determinate ways by its environment. Form in things natural is thus shown to have two complementary characters: it is internally dynamic and it is environmentally stimulated and conditioned.

### THE OPERATION OF APPETENCE

Turning from the description of appetence to an analysis of the way in which it operates, we find that certain distinctions must be made between functions which are natural to a given organism and the organic states which are involved in these functions. First of all it is essential to see just what a living being does, if one is to arrive at an accurate view of the powers, or faculties, of the organism. If it is desired to know what the thinking or sensitive faculty is, for example, it must first be asked what it is to think and to feel; it is perfectly obvious that an animal cannot perform functions for which it has not the capacity, but the capacity of itself cannot be independently investigated. Since the nutritive soul is basic for all animal life and therefore the most general aspect of the human soul, Aristotle discusses its powers first: they are to reproduce and to use food (Da, 415a). In another passage (Ha, 589a) these functions are given dominant place in the life of animals, as the center of their activities.

Each of these two passages also introduces the distinction which we have mentioned between functions and the organic states which are involved in them. These functions are "natural" to the organism, as basic to life; and "whatsoever is in conformity with nature is pleasant, and all animals pursue pleasure in keeping with their nature" (Ha, 589a). The using of food is natural, because the growth of the organism depends on such materials as constitute the various parts. In the former passage (Da, 415a, b) reproduction is said to be natural to the organism because all living beings strive to participate in the eternal and divine, through the perpetuation of the form which is theirs.

We have therefore a fundamental characteristic of natural functions: they are pleasant. And we have a fundamental characteristic of the appetence of an organism: it strives for that which is pleasant according to its nature. The use of the words "pleasure" and "pleasant" opens up a whole new field of inquiry—the organic states which are involved in the performance of natural functions, and therefore in the striving which brings about their performance. Aristotle classes as "affections" or "passions" of the soul, thinking, sensation, desire, and the activities which we call emotions. He proceeds cautiously and, without dogmatically making a universal statement, says that it seems probable that all such passive states of the soul are in common with the body. He cites anger, gentleness, fear, pity, courage, joy, loving, and hating as instances of affections which are suffered at the same time that the body is affected. The evidence which he gives is that at times anger or fear are not expressed, though strong and obvious conditions are present which ordinarily produce them; and, on the other hand, there are times when the organism is moved by causes that are small and not easily seen. He then cites a case which he considers an even more obvious example of the mutuality of the bodily and psychical aspects of emotion: sometimes when no condition is present which ordinarily is associated with fear, individuals are still affected with fear. This is an example of the penetrating insight Aristotle displays in his analysis of human behavior. These facts are explained today in terms of the effect which organic conditioning has upon the way an organism will respond to the stimulations of the environment, it being well established that even in some of the simplest reflexes the organic state affects the result of an external mechanical stimulus. Aristotle reasons from these phenomena that the affections of the soul are ideas immersed in matter (λόγοι ἔνυλοι) (Da, 403a). The meaning of this appears to be that a state, which we ordinarily identify as a specific kind of affection of the soul, typically arises in situations sufficiently characteristic that they can be described and classified as the normal context of that state. This particular aspect of the relation between the subject and his environment is a "λόγος"—the kind of λόγος which is typical of the appropriate affection. But it does not become an affection unless the body of the organism is in such condition that it responds in the typical manner. When it does, then the λόγος is "ἔνυλος"—the idea is, to translate literally, "enmattered."

This analysis shows how primary is the actual condition of the organism in emotional phenomena, considered as one kind of affection. But it also shows that the "idea" of such a state has an external reference, even if it so happens that it is not produced by an external cause. Aristotle further emphasizes this aspect of emotions by his definition of anger, which he gives to illustrate the necessity of this kind of reference: to be angry, or to be angered, "must be defined as a movement made by a body in a particular state, or by a part, or by a capacity of such a body roused by such a cause, with such an end in view" (Da, 403a). He then distinguishes the natural philosopher's definition of anger, as a boiling up of blood and heat around the heart, from that of the logician, as a craving for retaliation or something similar. One of these gives an account of the matter, the other of the form (εἶδος), that is, the inward nature or idea (λόγος) of the emotion.

Pleasure is to be considered in connection with the operation of appetence, as a phenomenon closely related to all the affections of the soul. We have seen that "whatsoever is in conformity with nature is pleasant, and all animals pursue pleasure in keeping with their nature" (Ha, 589a). In the *Ethics* pleasure is defined as an unimpeded activity according to nature (EN, 1153a). It is spoken of in both these passages as an end; yet while it may be pursued as an end, it is seen to be associated with the unimpeded functioning of natural capacities. It differs from the emotions chiefly in this, that while they have specific kinds of context in which they typically appear and which define the end of action to which they point, to be pleased is a reaction of the living being as a whole, which appears in the context of any unimpeded activity which is in accordance with the individual's nature or acquired character (EN, 1099a). It is the quality of organic response which accompanies the fulfillment or actualization of the individual's powers. Pain, as the opposite of pleasure, is the quality of organic response which is made to circumstances which bring sensory discomfort or frustrate the action which is natural to the individual (EN, 1117b).

Aristotle considers the complications which arise from conflicting motives or ends of action. One appetite may be opposed to or incompatible with another appetite. One instance of this takes place when contrary impulses are simultaneously stimulated, which is sometimes due to an individual's taking pleasure in things which are not pleasant in their own nature, but rather because of the character of the individual (EN, 1099a). The use of food is pleasant by nature and does not conflict with other goods. But gluttony is not primarily the use of food, but the indulgence of an artificial appetite which will conflict with the end of good health. If one finds his pleasure in things which are naturally pleasant, this particular kind of conflict will not arise.

Another type of conflict arises from the opposition between a present good and a future one whose claims are urged by the mind (νοῦς) (Da, 433b, f.). The quality of experience which is produced by the craving for an immediate good is different from that produced by the prospect of one in the future. But the moving cause is of one form in both cases: appetence is directed to an end which in one instance may be reached now, and in the other instance must be delayed to the future. The latter kind of behavior distinguishes man from the lower animals as one who is capable of intelligent response to a stimulus which is not temporally present, in preference to one which is. The mind, by thinking of this future end, furnishes the stimulation to appetence which secures this restraint of action toward the present goal in favor of the more distant one. But the question still remains, *why* will the mind do this? We shall delay its consideration until we come to a discussion of choice.

Besides this function of the mind in stimulating appetence with respect to remote ends, there are two further ways in which thinking affects activity. We have seen that the operations of the practical mind devise or discover appropriate means to reach the goal to which appetence is directed. In this way it facilitates movement, by marking out the path of activity. Reflection can, however, delay rather than facilitate movement. Just as in speculative inquiry one premise is often suppressed, so in practical reasoning an obvious minor premise is often not considered at all (Dma, 701a). Action which is performed without reflection is done quickly, through the actualizing of appetence without its being "sicklied o'er with the pale cast of thought."

The activities which are commonly called willing and choosing have always been of psychological interest. Aristotle describes the factors which are involved in setting an organism into motion in the passages of *De anima* and *De motu animalium* which have been discussed. It is in the *Ethics,* however, that we find a detailed analysis of "voluntary action" as a definite aspect of the initiation of movement, as the analysis of such powers is necessary for the adequate description of what constitutes character.

The first distinction which we notice is that between voluntary (τὰ ἑκούσια) and involuntary acts (τὰ ἀκούσια) (EN, 1110, f.). An act is involuntary under two conditions: (1) when it is performed under compulsion; or (2) when it is performed in ignorance. In the latter case Aristotle introduces another term, "not voluntary," (τὸ οὐχ ἑκούσιον) but if the agent regrets the action on becoming aware of its true nature, then the act is to be classified as involuntary—a term signifying that the action is against rather than without the willing of the individual.

The distinction between the involuntary acts of compulsion and voluntary acts is in the location of their origin (ἀρχή). When an agent acts under compulsion, more strictly speaking he is a patient being acted upon, since the origin of the act is outside himself, and he contributes nothing to it. But if the origin is within himself and he is adequately acquainted with the various issues which are involved, then the action is voluntary. It may be prompted by the heat of anger or desire, but is voluntary none the less.

Within the class of voluntary acts comes "προαίρεσις," which it is impossible to render in a convenient English expression. It is an intelligent, deliberated response to a total situation involving the object of desire (EN, 1111b–1113a). We shall use the term "intelligent response" as a translation, meaning thereby a considered response, which profits by past experience, to a situation which concerns the future, near or far. Sudden acts may thus be voluntary, if they are not initiated under compulsion, but they are not intelligent responses. Aristotle differentiates this kind of response from desire, passion, wish, and opinion. It cannot be identified with desire or passion, since even the lower animals, incapable of deliberation, act from these; as does also the man who is not adequately self-restrained. It is not wish, for one may wish for that which is either in itself impossible or not within the power of the individual to secure. Such things can be wished for but cannot be the objects of intelligent response. Neither is it opinion, which is characterized as true or false, whereas one responds intelligently concerning that which is good or bad. Furthermore, as with wish, opinion can be concerned with the impossible or with the eternal, which are not the objects of deliberation. The derivation of προαίρεσις makes these distinctions more significant. It signifies the taking of one thing before or in preference to something else, and, as thus defined, it is advisable to distinguish it from these other phenomena with which it might be confused.

Since intelligent response is a voluntary act which takes place after deliberation, it becomes necessary to inquire into the scope of things about which one deliberates (EN, 1112a, b). Aristotle names a number of things regarding which one does not deliberate and then concludes that deliberation takes place concerning (1) that about which the issue is in doubt; (2) that which is within one's control; (3) that which can be attained by action; (4) the means, not the end of an act. By this last characteristic it would appear that deliberation is essentially identical with the operation of what Aristotle terms the practical mind. There is a further likeness between his descriptions of deliberation and practical reasoning which is crucially important. We have seen how the practical mind is not something apart from either the goal of activity or the organism itself—it is rather that which connects the two. Its origin is the end which is sought, and its last step is identical with the first movement to take place toward the goal. The object of deliberation, on the other hand, is identical with that to which one responds intelligently, with the further explanation that by the time this response takes place, the action which ensues has already been determined (in the literal sense of bounded or marked off) by the course which deliberation has taken. The culmination of deliberation, therefore, is identical with the response. This pattern is so completely similar to that in which the definition of the last step of the practical mind is the first step of action that we are justified in saying that Aristotle thought of intelligent response not as an act which in any way can be isolated, but as the conclusion of a sequence of rationally causative factors. He sums up by saying that man is the origin of his actions—a conclusion which necessarily follows from the fact that deliberation, which issues in intelligent response, has to do not with ends but with means to reach ends, which are those of the individual. Action, therefore, will be determined not by some act of volition which can be isolated, but by what the man himself is, in the totality of his character.

This nature of intelligent response is further seen from the argument that when the doing of a thing comes from within, the not doing it has the same origin. This is to substantiate Aristotle's claim that virtue and vice are equally voluntary (EN, 1113b). It may be that here and now a man cannot do otherwise than he does, either through ignorance or through, say, a habit of carelessness. Yet the action must be classed as voluntary, if the failure to gain the appropriate knowledge or to develop a habit of carefulness sprang from past voluntary actions. Aristotle cites the objection that this placing of responsibility upon the individual involves a regress to birth, so that to be virtuous a man needs to be born with the knowledge of the right end. He cannot settle the point, but proposes that at least virtue and vice are equally voluntary, whatever their ultimate conditions may be. He further shows that our dispositions are not voluntary in the same sense as our actions (EN, 1114b, f.). We control our actions throughout their course, whereas in the development of habits of mind, we control the beginnings, but they acquire a momentum of their own which is largely imperceptible to us.

We have seen in our previous discussion that appetence can produce movement contrary to knowledge, and that at times there is a conflict arising from the incompatibility of a present goal to which appetence is directed with one which reflection suggests as preferable. In the *Ethics* further attention is directed to the question of whether or not a man will fail in self-restraint when he knows what he does to be wrong (EN, 1146b–1147b). On the surface of things, it appears clear that sometimes men who know what is right do wrong. But Aristotle seeks to show that it is only in certain senses that these men have knowledge. For example, a man may know a given thing which should be a factor in present action, yet that knowledge may not be thought of at present. Or a man may have knowledge of a universal which is involved in the case at hand, but fail to discern that this is a particular instance of that universal. Indeed, two universals may be involved, and the man may have knowledge of both universals and one particular, but fail to see the application through not perceiving the other particular. The example cited is that one may know that dry food is good for every man and that certain food is dry food (taken as a second universal). He also knows that he is a man (particular of the first universal), but fails to perceive that this food is of the certain kind that is dry (particular of the second universal). Again, sometimes knowledge is merely verbal, such as displayed by a man asleep, mad, or drunk, when he might repeat words without grasping their meaning. Finally, two universals may be opposed: on the one hand, a universal judgment may be present to the man's mind, which forbids certain action, of which he recognizes the one contemplated as a particular instance; but another universal judgment may affirm the pleasantness of action of a certain class, of which the one contemplated is a particular instance. Therefore, if desire is by chance present at the same time, it will lead to the forbidden action. Thus while knowledge is important in directing activity, it cannot determine action apart from desire.

An interesting distinction is made between vehemence and weakness as two forms of unrestraint—an important distinction in viewing the way in which voluntary action of a defective character takes place (EN, 1150b, f.). The vehement will act on passion, not waiting to deliberate. The weak, however, swerve because of passion from a course on which they have deliberated. Aristotle considers the former better than the latter, as such men do not yield to smaller temptations after deliberation, as do the weak sort of unrestrained men. The distinction serves to show how a given action may spring either from a strong impulse being unopposed or from the opposing factors being too feeble to be effective.

This analysis of acts of willing and responding intelligently leads to certain rather clear conclusions with regard to Aristotle's view of man's capacity to determine his own action. Aristotle's purpose and method save him from an immense amount of difficulty over which others have been compelled to labor. For he never discusses abstract faculties as such; he finds out first what actually goes on, and then concludes in a very common-sense way that what an individual does he has the capacity for doing. Therefore he never asks: "does man have freedom of will?" That he acts is plain; Aristotle's task becomes, therefore, an analysis of the factors which are involved in that activity. All activity has an origin. What is its *locus?* If external, then willing is not involved in the act. If internal, then the act is voluntarily performed, and what is meant by voluntary action must be analyzed for the various factors which it involves.

It becomes clear as we proceed that we are not concerned with freedom in the sense of the power to make arbitrary decision. The essential question is not, can a man do what is better or what is worse? It is, rather, can he do that which is better against strong appetitive forces? In any actual situation, there is what may be called the highest good to be secured if possible. Some men will attain it; some men will fall short, with varying degrees of failure. Aristotle is not concerned with the academic question as to whether or not all these kinds of men are endowed with "freedom of will." His question remains here, as elsewhere, *why* does this particular man do as he does? What are the factors involved in his reaching the goal or in his falling short of it? Putting the question this way calls for immediate recognition of the fact that in any situation the highest good is something complex and more remote from the claims of immediate appetites. There is never any such thing as unmotivated behavior. There is always the *why* of activity. Differences in behavior are according to whether a man responds to the immediate, narrow environmental context, or to more remote, larger environmental contexts.

To use our term "freedom," we may say that three types of action are recognized by Aristotle, two of them being capable of subdivision into many degrees. There is entire absence of freedom in the performance of involuntary acts under external compulsion. There is freedom from this kind of compulsion in the performance of the voluntary acts of the unrestrained man—the man who is impelled by the immediate claims of appetite, either through the vehemence of his nature leading him to action directed by passion without having deliberated, or through his weakness leading him to such action in spite of deliberation. But the highest degree of freedom is that which characterizes the action of the self-restrained man—the one whose character is so organized that the immediate claims of appetence are held in abeyance in order to secure a higher good. He is still activated by appetence, but appetence has been directed in harmony with reflection to fix upon more remote objects. These degrees of freedom, then, swing through an arc from external compulsion to inward discipline; they describe the factors which are involved in the field of willing and responding intelligently in a way which illuminates the whole process and furnishes a scientific basis for those who are concerned with the development of character. To the question, is man endowed with some measure of arbitrary freedom, Aristotle has no answer, as it is aside from the purpose of his inquiry.

### SUMMARY

The discussion of this chapter shows that the initiating and directing of activity involve many factors which can be distinguished for the purposes of analysis, but which are thoroughly entangled in any actual situation. They can be summarized schematically as follows:

1. Every action is controlled by its end, which, to the individual, is a good.

2. This end is that upon which is fixed the appetence of the individual; unless the goal which is presented by the environment is such that appetence is aroused, it will be powerless to motivate the organism.

3. The mind of the organism engages in deliberation on ways and means to attain this goal.

4. This process of deliberation may be immensely complicated. It may lead to considerations which nullify the claims of the goal. But if it reaches its end, that conclusion is the conclusion of the individual, for the mind is the organism thinking, rather than something apart from it. Thus the conclusion of this mental activity is identical with the actualizing or energizing of the individual in relation to his object, and the overt activity is in progress.

5. Involved in all this behavior are the affections of the soul, which are the organic expressions of the indi-

vidual's relation to the environmental context; and the feelings of pleasure and pain associated with the unimpeded or thwarted performance of the functions which are concerned.

6. The organization of habits of mind, or dispositions, is involved in determining whether a man in his voluntary behavior will through unrestraint respond to the simple, immediate environmental context or whether through self-restraint he will respond to the larger, more remote contexts.

*Chapter Four*

# THE CRITICAL ACTIVITIES OF THE ORGANISM

THE ENVIRONMENTAL and organic factors which are involved in the production of movement have occupied our attention in the foregoing chapter. We turn now to activities of a different order, which, however, in actual process, are not found apart from appetence, which we have considered as a cause of movement. The various activities can be separated for purposes of discussion; but it is always the individual who acts, and in any activity a complexity of factors can be distinguished.

The activities of the organism are instrumental to its satisfaction. It is aroused to action by appetence, and there is a sense in which the ensuing activity is for the purpose of satisfying this desire. In another sense, however, it is not desire which is satisfied, but the individual whom the desire has aroused. When consideration passes beyond this stage, the analysis of the consequent activity shows its instrumental nature very clearly. In the animals which do not have a rational soul, the primary capacity which remains to be considered is that of sensation, since the capacities for movement and sensation constitute that in which those things which have soul most radically differ from those which do not (Da, 403b). The power of reason must be added as the distinctive mark of the human soul, so that the activity of man may be described in terms of movement, sensation, and thought.

The activities of sensing and thinking (taken here in a very general sense) are functions of a general capacity which Aristotle describes as the critical, or judging, or discriminating capacity (τὸ κριτικόν) (Da, 432a). What he means by this is readily seen by his general view of the organism's interaction with its environment. The environment affects the individual in many ways, and the specific activities of sensing and thinking are the discriminating responses of the organism to the various traits of the world which environs it.

## SENSING

Sensing is the first activity of the organism which is aroused by the environment, making it the most essential of the capacities, any one of which implies the presence of life (Da, 413a, b). Without it, response to the environment would be impossible, and this is precisely that which characterizes living things. As this is the function of sensation, touch is the primary sense, so that all animals share in this capacity (Da, 413b, Dpa, 653b).

Sensing is directly related to appetence, and in two ways —or it could be said that its relation to appetence is circular. The presence of sensation always arouses some kind of desire, for what is sensed causes pleasure or pain, and desire is a craving for what is pleasant (Da, 413b, 414b, 431a).

But not only is sensing instrumental to the stimulation of appetence—it is instrumental to its satisfaction as well. Touch is essential to all animals, making possible an adjustment to surrounding objects, even for those organisms which do not move (Da, 413b). The other senses, while not necessary for life, are essential for the activities of more complexly organized life, which of course would not be possible without them (Da, 434b).

The faculty of sensation is always a function of the environment, as well as of the organism, and consequently has, in itself, only potential and not actual existence. The senses themselves do not give rise to sensation. They are powers of the organism to be stimulated in certain ways, and this stimulation must be present to produce actual sensing (Da, 416b, f.). Sensation is an experience of the individual by means of specialized organs of the body, each of which Aristotle thought to be a homogeneous part. This was on the ground that each sense had to do with one kind of sensible object, and, since that which is acted upon must be potentially similar to that which is acting upon it, the sense organ must also be simple in nature (Dpa, 647a). Besides these specialized sense organs, there is a general center in or around the heart for both movement and sensation, so that a means exists for the coördination of the separate activities (Dpa, 647a, 681b; Dsv, 456a). This appears to be Aristotle's explanation in physiological terms of sensation (αἴσθησις) as a general power of the organism, as distinct from a sense organ (αἰσθητήριον). Sensation is an activity by means of sense organs, rather than an activity merely *of* the sense organs. Sensation is a movement which penetrates to the soul (Da, 408b); again, he cites the fact that when a blow is struck on the temple in such a way as to sever the passages connected with the eye, blindness results immediately, to prove that the experience of sensation is not at the surface of the eye but is within (Dss, 438b). That is, sensation is never an isolated activity, but is always involved in the total activity of the organism—the soul.

The stimulus which arouses sensation is always a particular object, wherein may be seen the difference between sensing and knowing (Da, 417b). One cannot sense squareness, for example. He may sense a square table or a square figure, but squareness as a universal is an object of knowledge, not of sensation. Another way of stating the difference is that the sensation is a response to an object whose actual existence is always external to the organism, whereas the universals are actualized only in the soul itself. What Aristotle means by this will become clearer when we consider in detail the various thinking processes. This distinction between sensing and knowing, in terms of their respective objects, explains, too, why it is that one can think whenever one wishes to, but one cannot sense without the presence of the external object.

It has become customary to make a distinction between sensation and "perception," in terms of the activity of the mind with respect to the sense data. In contrast with this method, Aristotle's view of the contextual continuity between the environment and the powers of the organism led him to make the relevant distinctions in terms of the various aspects of the objects of sensation. He thus distinguishes three meanings of the term "object sensed" (Da, 418a). In two of them sensation is of the object itself; in the third, sensation is of something incidental to the object. Of objects sensed in themselves, some stimulate only one sense, such as color or sound; others, such as movement, rest, number, shape, and size, are discriminated by the several senses. That which is sensed as something incidental to the object itself is illustrated in the sensing of a white object as the son of Diares; "the son of Diares" is only incidentally sensed, the object itself being the white color. The second and third of these meanings of "object sensed" show how immediately the activity of thinking is interwoven with the activity of sensing. They can be abstractly considered, but raw sensation rarely exists in isolation, as the organism is ordinarily responding not to the isolated simple stimulations of the special senses, but to that which is incidental to these stimulations. Or to state the case more aptly, the organism is usually responding to the object to which the simple sensory stimulations are incidental.

Aristotle gave close attention to the way in which the external objects actually affect the organism. In seeing, hearing, and smelling it is clear that, as the object is at a distance, there must be some medium for the stimulus to reach the sense organ. With touch and taste the case is not so clear, but Aristotle concludes that a medium exists for them too, though there is a considerable difference between them as sensing that which is close at hand, and the other three capacities for sensing that which is at a distance. In each case there is a unique stimulus, acting in or through a medium upon a specialized organ of sense whose nature it is to be affected by such a stimulus.

The object of vision is color, which has the definite location of the surface of an object, which is so constituted that it is, in itself, visible, although visibility need not be part of its essence (Da, 418a). This color could never affect the eye were there not something between; that is why Democritus was wrong in asserting that, were "the between" empty, even an ant in the sky would be clearly visible. Something evidently must exist in the intervening space, and Aristotle calls this "the transparent." A proof of the necessity of this is the impossibility of seeing anything when placed too close to the eye. It seemed evident to Aristotle that something transparent really existed—something through which things could appear and without which things would not appear. Air and solid objects, such as water, are transparent not because of what is essential to them as water, air, and so forth, but because they have a certain natural attribute which is also common to the eternal body above (Da, 418a, b).

To return to our original object of vision, which is color: we find that its essential nature is to produce movement in the transparent, when the latter has been actualized as light by some source of illumination. Darkness is the transparent in a potential condition, and light is this actuality of the transparent. It is the light as modified by color—the movement effected by color in the previously actualized transparent which exists in "the between"—which directly acts upon the organ of sight and gives rise to vision of the color (Da, 418b, f.).

There is a significant difference between vision and hearing with respect to the original stimulus. Color is something which is present on the surface of the object seen, whose essential nature is to produce movement in the already actualized transparent. But there is nothing corresponding to this in the case of objects which produce sound. To press closely Aristotle's analysis of objects sensed into three classes, there is no object which in itself is sensed in the case of sound. For the sound is not something which is in the object itself, except as the object is capable of producing it in the medium. Indeed, Aristotle says that sound is either potential or actual, meaning that such things as bronze, which have potential sound, are capable of producing it. But clearly potential sound has by no means the same status as color, since there must be a movement between two bodies, in which they are struck together, to produce the sound. Sound, then, is an activity of the appropriate medium, air. It occurs when things which are suitably smooth and flat, or hollow, are struck by another body. The smoothness is a condition for the air remaining continuous, and the flatness or hollowness is the condition which allows the compacting and vibrating of the air (Da, 419b, f.).

The organ of hearing must be capable of receiving these vibrations of the air, and Aristotle finds this to be possible because of the air in the ear. It is deeply enclosed, so that the imparted motion will not be lost; in fact the spirals of the ear so protect the air that one can hear in water, as the water does not fully penetrate (Da, 420a).

Another significant characteristic of sound is that the organism can produce it as well as sense it (Da, 420b, f.). In this it differs from vision—we shall pass over the senses of smell, *et al.*, without comment in this regard. We have noticed in the account of the organism's development how one structure will serve different functions. In a similar way animals that breathe do so for a definite physiological purpose, but the air is also used for the production of voice. Not every sound produced by a living being—as a cough, for example—is voice. Rather, voice is sound which the organism uses as a sign, to communicate meaning. In this department of sense, therefore, we find that the organism is equipped both to be acted upon by the environment and to act upon it, through the same medium.

The two senses of sight and hearing are of importance for all of life, each one contributing more than the other in certain respects. For the requirements of adjustment in the environment to promote the basic necessities of life, sight is the more important, for all bodies have color, whereas sound is much less useful in discriminating ordinary objects. But it is through the spoken word that instruction is received, and so hearing contributes to intelligence more than sight. For this reason those who are blind from birth are more intelligent than those born deaf and dumb. However, this contribution of hearing is only incidental, for it is not the sound itself which thus contributes to intelligence, but the words of speech in their capacity as symbols. This is in contrast with vision, where color is in itself a part of the object which it signifies, rather than being an incidental product (Dss, 437a).

Aristotle finds it harder to give an account of smell, because its conditions are more obscure than is the case with sight and hearing. This sense in man is much less discriminating than it is with the lower animals, and, because it has such a low power of discrimination, it is impossible to experience the sensation without being aware that it is pleasant or unpleasant. Nothing is said about the sense organ itself, except that it is stimulated through a medium, such as air or water. Animals which inhale smell only in the act of inhaling, as if the organ were uncovered in this process, as the eye is uncovered in order to see. But just as some animals do not have a covering for the eyes, evidently those which do not inhale do not have this covering of the organ of smell, so that they are affected by smell without inhaling. Aristotle, identifying smell with the objects which produce it, cites the destruction of non-inhaling animals by strong smells, such as bitumen and sulphur, as evidence that these animals do have a sense of smell (Da, 421a, b, f.).

The senses of taste and touch are alike in that there is no medium outside the body, as is the case with the three senses we have considered. Flavor never exists except in a liquid, or what can become wet, such as salt. Consequently the sense organ for taste must be something potentially but not actually liquid. This condition is fulfilled when the tongue is neither dry nor too wet, in neither of which conditions can it taste (Da, 422a, b).

The sense of touch is not the same as that of taste, since there are parts of the body which have the sensation of touching which do not taste. In each case the absence of a foreign body in the place of a medium makes it appear that no medium exists. But Aristotle argues that if a thin membrane surrounded the body, one would experience touch just as quickly as if it were not present, and he concludes that whereas the sense organs for seeing, hearing, and smelling are acted upon *by* a medium, the sense organs of taste and touch are acted upon *through* and at the same time as the medium, as when a man is wounded through his shield. The flesh, then, is not the sense organ, but the medium which is affected by the object of taste or touch simultaneously with the sense organs, which are within the flesh (Da, 422b–424a).

We have noted that Aristotle places touch in the position of first importance among the senses, as the only one necessary to life. He further believed that while man was inferior to the lower animals with respect to the other senses, he was superior to most with respect to touch. This is involved in his being the most intelligent of living beings, as is shown by the fact that men are more or less endowed with intelligence in proportion to their capacity for touch, as is the case with no other sense; men of soft skin and flesh are more intelligent than those of hard (Da, 421a)—a possible comfort for those who tend to have "the double sort of chin."

Is there a special sense organ in the case of objects such as movement, rest, number, and so forth, which are shared by the several senses? Aristotle's answer is that there is a common sensation of these common objects; this is not due to a special sense organ, nor again is it merely incidental to any of the other senses. In a genuine sense these are common sensibles, and their stimulation of the organism is not exactly in the pattern of the incidental stimulation through one sense organ by the proper object of another. That is, sensing movement by any one of the senses is not like sensing bile by sight. This latter is due to the past experience of simultaneous stimulation of sight and taste by yellow and bitter, so that these two senses have acted together as one, asserting one object. But movement can be sensed by one sense, regardless of past association. Since this is true, the common sensibles are more readily distinguished; were they found only in connection with vision, for example, color and magnitude might appear to be one, but, since magnitude exists in the objects of other senses, it is readily distinguished (Da, 425a, b). Indeed Aristotle implies that the multiple sensing of these objects is a major function of having more than one sense. This emphasis on their importance is supported by the primacy given to quantitative considerations in the scientific movements of modern time.

Aristotle's method in this inquiry illustrates clearly the difference between his view of knowledge and certain historically important doctrines. Locke, for example, called these common sensibles the primary qualities of bodies, meaning thereby the qualities which, in themselves, are in the bodies and are inseparable from them, as distinguished from secondary qualities, which are in bodies only as powers to produce sensations by the primary qualities. The various stimulations which come from objects are received by the various senses, and the problem for Locke was how these various sense data were transformed into a relevant idea of the whole object. Aristotle's inquiry is pointed in the other direction. The organism senses the whole object—in fact, one sense is equal to the task. He does not consider as a problem this one sensation of a whole object; his question is, rather, how can the various aspects of the object be discriminated? The answer is found in the variety of sense organs, which furnishes not only the wealth of specific stimulations which could not otherwise be received, but also the means—by the faculty of sensing, of which the senses are specific instruments—of isolating the important aspects of the object, which he called the common sensibles.

A similar question relates to the way in which we apprehend the difference between the objects of different senses, such as white and sweet. It must be by sense, since these are sensible objects. It is impossible to judge them different by different senses, for no standard of judgment would exist, as when two different people sense objects. Aristotle here appeals to the unity of the judging faculty, and finds the possibility of judging things different to be due to the fact that the judging capacity is numerically indivisible, but divided in essence; that, as divisible, it senses divided things, but is indivisible otherwise (Da, 426b, f.).

How are we aware of our sensations? It is necessary either that sight senses that it sees or that some other sense does so. The latter would involve an infinite regress, since then a third sense would be equally necessary to apprehend the second, and so on. Aristotle assumes, therefore, that awareness of sensation arises with the first sense (Da, 425b).

These details of Aristotle's description of sensation have been given to show how this entire field of organic activity fits into his fundamental doctrine of behavior as explicable only in terms of interaction between an organism and its environment. His summary statements on the nature of sensation bring this out very clearly, when considered against the background of the detailed analysis. Sensing, he says, is the receiving of the form of sensible objects without the matter (Da, 424a). This is precisely what gives a sense organ its character, as distinguished from other bodily structures—it is a part which has this capacity of discriminating the form of objects from their matter. Plants do not have sensation because they lack this power and are affected simultaneously by the matter and form of things which touch them. This is why an excess of sensed objects renders the sense organs inoperative—the imparted movement being too strong, the form is broken up.

This receiving of the forms of external objects by the sense organs involves a continuity between the organism and its environment which Aristotle states in the strongest terms. The activity of the sensed objects and of the sensation itself is one and the same, although their essence is not. That is, for example, the thing sounding and the thing hearing are two different things—their essence is not the same. But the sounding and the hearing are continuous; to use Aristotle's terms, they are the same activity. Since acting and being acted upon are in the thing acted upon, and since sensation is the acting of the environment upon the organism, both the sound and the actual hearing are in the potential hearing; Aristotle relates this to his principle that it is not necessary for the thing which causes motion to be moved. Since the activity of that which is sensed and the activity of the organ sensing are thus the same, the two members of each pair—sound and hearing, flavor and taste, and so on—must exist and be destroyed simultaneously (Da, 425b, f.). Sensation is a joint function of environmental activity and organic capacity.

## THINKING

We turn now to "thinking," using the word in a general sense to denote the non-sensory activities of the critical, discriminating, or judging capacity. Aristotle points out that since both sensation and thought are functions of the soul in which it discriminates and has knowledge of existing things, they had been taken by some of the older philosophers to be the same. This makes it impossible to explain error (a serious defect in view of its being more natural to living creatures and occupying more of their time) and was the basis of the doctrine that all appearances are true. When these two activities are separated, however, it is seen that the sensing of particular things is always true, but that thinking is often false; all living beings sense things truly, but it belongs only to rational animals to err in reason (Da, 427a, b)—which reminds us of Aristotle's citing the capacity of wind-eggs to rot as evidence that they possess life.

We have seen that sensation is closely linked to appetence, and the same is true of thought. The soul does not move the living being by mechanical force, as Democritus taught, but by the thinking processes issuing in the response of the organism (Da, 406b), in the way which we have described in Chapter III. In this production of movement, thought is linked with sensation in the arousal of appetence; images arise in the thinking capacity of the soul, and when the soul asserts that something is good or evil in connection with these images, it avoids or pursues (Da, 431a).

The distinction between the potential and the actual is to be made with respect to thinking, just as it was in sensation. There are two ways, for example, in which a man may have knowledge potentially: he may have knowledge in the sense that he belongs to the class of beings which are capable of attaining knowledge, even if he has not yet learned; again, he may have an expert knowledge of grammar but be asleep or attending to his dinner. When the unlearned man learns, and the grammarian broods on his moods, then potential knowledge becomes actual.

The analysis of thinking shows it to be closely analogous to sensing. It is the being acted upon by the thing thought, or rather it is the receiving of the form of the thing thought.

This means that as a power of the organism and a part of the soul it must be potentially, though not actually, of the same character as the object of thought. This activity is what Aristotle calls the mind (νοῦς); and therefore the mind, as we saw was true of sensation, has no actual existence except when it is in operation. The mind is the place of forms, indeed, but these forms are not actualized except when thinking is taking place (Da, 429a). Hence it cannot be said that the mind thinks at times and at other times does not think (Da, 430a). In one way the thinking capacity is very different from the sensing; an excessive sensory stimulation destroys the power of sensation, but an intense thought renders the mind more able, rather than less, to think of inferior things. This is due to the bodily nature of sensation, as compared with the separable nature of mind (Da, 429a, b).

We have seen that Aristotle described sensation as the reception of the forms of sensible objects without their matter (Da, 424a). But mind is the place of potential forms, which are actualized in thinking (Da, 429a); while active sensing concerns particular things, knowledge is of universals, so that one can think when he wishes to, but cannot experience sensation without the presence of a sensible object (Da, 417b). How then do the forms of sensible objects, which are received by sense, differ from the forms which are the objects of thought?

The answer to this question shows not only how mind goes beyond sense, but how dependent mind is upon sense. In each case we have to do with things which are external to the organism and which affect the organism through sense. In sensation itself we found certain distinctions in terms of the object sensed (Da, 418a). This may be a particular thing, such as color, which affects one sense only; or it may be a common sensible such as magnitude; or it may be something which is only incidental to the sense datum, such as the son of Diares. These distinctions appear on analysis to present two characteristics: they represent varying degrees of simplicity in the sense data, so that when we come to sense the son of Diares the raw data of sense are considerably complicated by the various factors of the critical faculty as a whole, operating in the experience of the individual; but in each case, simple or complex, the object is particular. It is this color, white; or this magnitude, three inches by five inches; or this man, the son of Diares. The white body, or the object of a given size, or the man himself does not, of course, get into the eye. That is why Aristotle says that sensation is the reception of the form without the matter. But it is always the form of a particular.

It is at this point that the critical activity of mind (νοῦς), while depending upon all the activity of sense, nevertheless passes beyond it. As soon as the question is raised, what *is* color, or magnitude, or man, then we are no longer considering particulars and the forms of particulars, but universals. Without the sensed objects the questions could not be raised, but the mind goes beyond the sensed objects in its operations. Aristotle illustrates the difference by citing in explanation hot and cold as sensations with which flesh is involved. But what is fleshiness? "Straight" and "snub-nosed" always have to do with something straight or with noses. But what are straightness or snub-nosedness (Da, 429b)? These questions cannot be raised without the activity of sense, nor answered without the activity of mind.

Dombey and Son (Dickens, *Dombey and Son* chapter viii) had a clear perception of this distinction:

"Papa! what's money?"

. . .

Mr. Dombey was in a difficulty. He would have liked to give him some explanation involving the terms circulating-medium, currency, depreciation of currency, paper, bullion, rates of exchange, value of precious metals in the market, and so forth; but looking down at the little chair, and seeing what a long way down it was, he answered: "Gold, and silver, and copper. Guineas, shillings, half-pence. You know what they are?"

"Oh yes, I know what they are," said Paul. "I don't mean that, papa. I mean what's money after all."

. . .

"What is money after all!" said Mr. Dombey, backing his chair a little, that he might the better gaze in sheer amazement at the presumptuous atom that propounded such an inquiry.

And then little Paul, as if to show that he was a congenital Aristotelian, and a master of the four causes, asked:

"I mean, papa, what can it do?"

We have seen that thinking, as a part or function of the soul, is potentially, though not actually, of the same character as the object of thought (Da, 429a). In two other passages it appears definitely that when the mind is actually thinking, it is identical with the object thought (Da, 429b, f.); and that knowledge (ἐπιστήμη) actualized is identical with its object (Da, 430a). It would indeed be hard to go further in asserting a thoroughgoing intimacy between the organism and its environment than in this theory of thought and knowledge. Mind is the thinking process itself, knowledge is the knowing process itself: it would be true to Aristotle's total picture to say that the mind is the organism thinking. And so completely continuous is the organic-environmental context that the objects of the environment themselves, not in matter but in form, are the very stuff of thought. The particular things are actualized in a particular time and space; the forms and universals which are involved in these very particulars may be actualized in as many minds as you please. There is thus a sense in which there is a great unity in the thinking which occurs in the universe, but this unity is grounded not in Absolute Thought, but in the one order of particular things in Nature. That we are not going too far in this statement of Aristotle's thought is shown by his treatment of the independence and separability of νοῦς. Thinking and speculating decay because the organism decays; thought itself, however, is unaffected (Da, 408b). The adequate explanation of this seemingly strange position is that νοῦς is not strictly a private affair. It is one aspect of the great order of nature: an aspect shared by organisms that have this highest of capacities.

The activity of the thinking mind, therefore, is to be explained not in its own terms but in terms of the intelligible world with which it is in continuity and reciprocity. Eventually, this forces Aristotle into a fluidity in the use of words which denote various mental activities. Presently we shall examine these expressions in their discriminating senses, but it is helpful at this point to note that the various terms are not, even by Aristotle himself, kept exclusively to their special denotations. They overflow and intermingle. The most outstanding example is νοῦς itself. After confining it by definition to the realm of universals, Aristotle comes to use it of the apprehension of particulars on which universals are based—which apprehension, indeed, is even termed sensation (EN, 1143b). Why will not the definitions stick? Because they are of words used to describe the activities of a mind which knows the intelligible world, and this world exhibits just that phenomenon. It is not a department store with sections 1 . . . n, but a great complexity, and the activities of the knowing mind are similarly complicated.

In differentiating thought from sensation, it has been noted that the sensing of particular things is always true, but that thinking may be false (Da, 427b). A few words more need to be said to present Aristotle's views on the nature of error. First, Aristotle modified the above statement in a later paragraph to allow just a little bit of error even in the sensing of particular things; no doubt this was on the basis of the natural imperfection to be expected in sense organs. Error is also found in sensation which is not of particular objects, as in judging whether a white object is one thing or another, and in discriminating common sensibles, such as movement and size (Da, 428b).

But within the mind itself there are also differences with respect to error. Imaginations may be false; indeed, most of them appear to be so (Da, 428a). Or things may have a false appearance, but our apprehension of them be correct, as in the case of the sun appearing to be a foot in width (Da, 428b). But, just as in sensation the sensing of particular objects is without error which is involved in the process as such, so there is one process of thought which is always true. This is when the mind (νοῦς) is dealing with the essence, or abstract nature of a thing, and not with some particular instance of it (Da, 430b). As soon as you have the particular instance, of course, you are dealing with that which is the object of sensation as well as of thought, and hence comes the possibility of error in sensing. But this would not be, strictly speaking, an error of thought, but of sensation. How then does mind err with respect to particular objects? The explanation is found in Aristotle's discussion of simple and combined concepts. Concerning indivisible units the mind does not err, and we may say that the essence or abstract nature of a thing is such an indivisible unit. But any particular instance of such a form combines with it certain relations in space and time which render it, as an object of thought, no longer a simple but a combined concept and hence liable to error (Da, 430a, b).

In our discussion so far we have used certain terms which have to do with the processes of thought, without critically examining them for their specific meanings. We shall now look into Aristotle's analysis of this total activity of mind and the specific terms which he employs to this end.

The kind of activity which is characteristic of man, as compared with the lower animals, we shall call rational conduct (πρᾶξις). Three powers of the soul govern this conduct: sensation (αἴσθησις), mind (νοῦς), and appetence (ὄρεξις) (EN, 1139a). In Chapter III we have examined appetence, and sensation has occupied our attention in the first part of the present chapter. It remains for us to examine the various aspects of mind (νοῦς). This term is used by Aristotle sometimes in a general sense, as we have done in the discussion so far, and sometimes in a specialized sense which we shall come to in the course of analysis.

A doctrine which has been set forth in the explanation of both sensing and knowing is the master principle of Aristotle's analysis of mind and its activities. Since there must be some sort of similarity between subject and object in knowing, the wide differences which exist in the objects of knowledge imply corresponding differences in the powers of the knower (EN, 1139a). These powers in themselves are by their very nature unobservable. We turn, then, to the objects with which they have to do and *what* they do with these objects, and here we have before us an objective field for a valid analysis of mind—which, let us remember, is actual only when it is engaged in this activity.

The first and most fundamental division of the rational power of the soul into two parts we have already had occasion to notice: first, the scientific (τὸ ἐπιστημονικόν) has as its object the things whose first principles are invariable; second, the calculative (τὸ λογιστικόν) deliberates about things which admit of variation (EN, 1139a).

Aristotle's concern in this analysis was to discover the contribution made by the various mental activities to a good life. Since virtue did not consist in isolated acts but rather in reliable habits, he inquired into the habits, dispositions, or conditions (ἕξεις) which constituted the respective virtues (or excellences) of the various aspects of mind. He found that there were five leading habits or conditions of mind by which the soul comes to the proof of truth: art, scientific knowledge, practical intelligence, wisdom, and theoretical intelligence (EN, 1139b). On examination the second, fourth, and fifth of these are found to be powers of the scientific function; the second and third are powers of the calculative. To anticipate the conclusion of the discussion, all the intellectual virtues are summed up under practical intelligence and wisdom (EN, 1143b).

Aristotle distinguishes between making and doing. The activity of art is engaged with making things, which differ in this respect from those things which come into existence of necessity or are constituted by nature. Art (τέχνη) as a habit of mind, therefore, is a disposition of the mind by which it reaches truth concerned with the activity of making, and lack of art is an opposite disposition, whose activity does not issue in reaching such practical truth (EN, 1140a).

Practical intelligence (φρόνησις) is defined as a rational habit by which the mind attains truth about action, concerning things which are good and bad for man, that is, which will promote both one's own welfare and that of mankind (EN, 1140b). This general virtue is, in turn, characterized by certain secondary habits or powers, which concern the same department of conduct. First is deliberative excellence (εὐβουλία) (EN, 1142a, b) which is correctness in thinking (διάνοια)—this is the power of devising an appropriate means to a good end and in a suitable time (EN, 1142b). A second characteristic of practical intelligence is comprehension (σύνεσις or εὐσυνεσία). It does not issue in commands, as does practical intelligence as a whole, but is rather the power of the mind to judge correctly concerning issues which arise in this field, primarily when the origin of their statement is from someone else (EN, 1142b, f.). The third of the secondary powers of practical intelligence is consideration (γνώμη, εὐγνωμοσύνη, or συγγνώμη), a disposition to examine sympathetically the affairs of others, to the end of action which will be suitable to the entire situation (EN, 1143a).

Aristotle's discussion of temperance (σωφροσύνη) as a requisite for practical intelligence involves the always interesting fact that persons who are never tempted to believe that twice two is three will nevertheless believe things as unreasonable when their pleasure is at stake—like the one who "simply didn't believe" that a slice of bread contained so many calories, so counted them as less in her reducing diet. Aristotle derived the word σωφροσύνη from two words meaning "to save" and "intelligence" and accounts for this construction of the word by the fact that temperance acts as "preserving intelligence." That is, pleasure and pain, while not perverting such apprehensions as are involved in mathematics, do throw one off course in the case of apprehensions which concern action. Temperance, therefore, is that which enables the individual to keep firm hold on the first principles of action, when otherwise this grasp of principle would be destroyed (EN, 1140b).

So far our discussion has concerned the habits or dispositions (ἕξεις) which constitute excellence or virtue of the calculative power (τὸ λογιστικόν). But the mind is exclusively a going concern, and therefore these excellences do not characterize the calculative power as such, but rather its many-sided activity. This activity can in turn be analyzed according to the various functions which it performs, and in discussing the dispositions, which are his chief concern for ethics, Aristotle uses distinguishing terms which express the different aspects of this total activity.

Imagination (φαντασία) occupied a very dubious place

in Aristotle's classification. It was neither sensation nor thought (διάνοια) (Da, 427b). Later (Da, 433a) it is admitted to the caste of thought by a kind of projected responsibility: "if . . . one regards imagination as some sort of thinking process (νόησις)." This is almost canceled immediately by attributing it not only to men, but also to other living beings in which there is neither thought (νόησις) nor calculation (λογισμός). It is safe to conclude that Aristotle thought of it as "some sort of thinking process," which we can, through this dubious classification, identify as the simplest form of mental activity. It is the process by which images (φαντάσματα) come to be in us (Da, 428a), images which are like objects of sense, except that they have no matter. As such, they are essential even to speculative thought (Da, 432a).

The next activity of the mind to be noticed is ὑπόληψις, of which "grasping" seems to be the best translation. It is used in connection with activities both of the scientific power and of the calculative (Da, 427b; EN, 1140b) to signify the taking into the mind of the facts of a situation as they are, without implying what the subsequent activity will be. In calculative thought grasping appears to furnish the data for the forming of opinion (δόξα), which is characterized as true or false and which has the power of affecting its possessor, as when one who has apprehended certain things forms the opinion that danger threatens (Da, 427b).

The comprehensive type of activity which characterizes the power we are considering is calculation (λογισμός), and Aristotle identifies this with deliberation (βούλευσις) (EN, 1139a), which carries with it the idea of sufficiently prolonged consideration of issues to serve as a basis for action.

In Chapter III we examined in detail the nature of deliberation and saw that it is consummated in intelligent response (προαίρεσις). This response marks the complete blending of thought and appetence in man who is himself the origin of his activity, for it is defined by Aristotle as the mind (νοῦς) fused with appetence or appetence fused with mind (διάνοια) (EN, 1139b).

Turning to Aristotle's analysis of the scientific power of the mind, we find the first disposition in which its excellence consists to be scientific knowledge (ἐπιστήμη). We know in this way things which do not admit of variation, and hence the activity characterized by this virtue concerns itself about things beyond the range of observation. If such unobserved things were objects rather of calculative activity, nothing could be known of them, since they might be subject to change when they were beyond observation. Objects of scientific knowledge, therefore, exist of necessity and hence are eternal. We know things scientifically by arriving at them deductively from first principles, which, though unproved, are held with complete certainty (EN, 1139b).

But how are these first principles come by? Certainly not by any of the calculative activities, since these have to do with variables. And not by scientific knowledge itself, for this is the disposition whereby we demonstrate deductively. It remains for theoretical intelligence (νοῦς, now used in the specific sense as distinct from that in which it designates the entire nonsensory critical faculty) to be the disposition whereby the mind apprehends first principles (EN, 1140b, f.).

The principal excellence of the scientific faculty and the capstone of all the intellectual virtues is wisdom (σοφία). Used in the best sense, this virtue characterizes not a master of a particular art, but an intelligent master in general. It combines theoretical intelligence whereby a man grasps first principles, with scientific knowledge or the conclusions which follow from the first principles. It is thus the "consummated knowledge of the most exalted objects" (EN, 1141a).

These three excellences, then, characterize the activity, which remains to be analyzed, of the scientific power. It has been noted that grasping (ὑπόληψις) is a term used to describe activity which is fundamental both to the scientific power and to the calculative. Examples of its use in connection with the former occur when Aristotle says that we all grasp that a thing which we know scientifically does not admit of variation (EN, 1139b) and that scientific knowledge is a grasping of universals and of things which are of necessity (EN, 1140b). It appears to be a term which Aristotle uses to signify a fundamental reception of objects in the mind, the differentiations to be made by other terms.

Knowledge (γνῶσις) is the general term denoting the result of such reception of objects in the mind, whether of the objects of the scientific power or of the calculative (EN, 1139a).

Another term (γνώρισις) designates an acquaintance with the principles which are used in the process of deduction as explanatory of a given conclusion—a conclusion which is then held with conviction (πίστις) (EN, 1139b). To know the conclusions which flow from the first principles in the reasoning of the wise man is expressed by the word εἰδέναι (EN, 1141a).

Two expressions remain which seem to designate processes which are exclusively involved in the functions of the scientific power. To learn (μανθάνειν) a thing is to come to comprehend it scientifically (EN, 1143a). Scientific knowledge can be taught, starting from facts previously known, and the obverse activity by which the objects of this kind of knowledge come to be known is learning (τὸ μανθάνειν) (EN, 1139b). It is of significance that Aristotle stressed the spoken word (λόγος) as the cause of learning (Dss, 437a), so that animals which are intelligent, but lack the sense of hearing, cannot be taught (Me, 980b). This view of learning (using the term in a more restricted sense than is the case in the treatment of memory) is not sufficiently developed by Aristotle from the standpoint of the way in which learning actually takes place, but is treated in terms of demonstration. If he had developed the implications of this dependence of learning upon spoken discourse, the outcome might well have been to consummate the critical activities of the mind in the vision which comes through the refinements of language rather than from something entirely separate from the organism. The νοῦς, which alone enters from outside (Dga, 736b), would then have arisen in the enterprise of discourse.

The remaining term which is used exclusively of activity within the scientific power is "seeing" or "beholding" (θεωρία) (EN, 1139a, 1143b, 1177a). As distinct from the mental reception of objects, or learning the objects of scientific knowledge, or knowing these things, or having a conviction based upon them, θεωρία, in its most specific meaning, is an active beholding of—well, of something which Aristotle did not make as clear as we might wish. But since, as this was the highest activity of man and we shall credit Aristotle himself with aspiring thereto, we might by beholding his life conclude that the essence of θεωρία is the beholding of the beauty and the order of nature.

This is the lofty end of rational conduct (πρᾶξις), which we found to involve sensation, appetence, and mind (νοῦς), whose activity (διάνοια) is a function of the scientific (τὸ ἐπιστημονικόν) and calculative (τὸ λογιστικόν) powers. Excellence in the functioning of the calculative power consists in the dispositions (ἕξεις) of art (τέχνη), and of practical intelligence (φρόνησις), with its requisite of temperance (σωφροσύνη) and its varieties of deliberative excellence (εὐβουλία), comprehension (σύνεσις), and consideration (γνώμη). These dispositions, in turn, involve the activities of the calculative power in imagination (φαντασία), grasping (ὑπόληψις), opinion (δόξα), calculation (λογισμός), deliberation (βούλευσις), and intelligent response (προαίρεσις). Excellence in the functioning of the scientific power (τὸ ἐπιστημονικόν) consists in the dispositions (ἕξεις) of scientific knowledge (ἐπιστήμη), of theoretical intelligence (νοῦς), and of wisdom (σοφία). These dispositions involve the activities of the scientific power in grasping (ὑπόληψις), knowledge (γνῶσις, γνώρισις, τὸ εἰδέναι), conviction (πίστις), learning (τὸ μανθάνειν), and beholding (θεωρία). It is to be emphasized again that the master principle governing Aristotle's analysis is the doctrine of similarity of character between the knower and the known; therefore, analysis of the powers of the mind rests upon the distinction of the various kinds of objects with which thinking has to do.

## REMEMBERING AND RECALLING

When the factor of time is explicitly considered in relation to the critical activities of the mind, the field of investigation is enlarged in an interesting way. That the activities which we have examined take place in the present is a truism. But we found the future to be involved in the activities of the practical mind: closely related to its very essence is the projection of activities into the future, with the evaluation of possible results. The past, too, is involved in the behavior of the organism, in and through its activities of remembering and recalling, which form one of the great fields of inquiry in psychology.

Aristotle differentiates learning (τὸ μανθάνειν), remembering (τὸ μνημονεύειν), and recalling (τὸ ἀναμιμνήσκεσθαι) in a way which is entirely familiar to modern usage. Remembering and recalling differ in that the first is a retaining of the effects of past experience, whereas the second is a recovering of knowledge and sensation, a process which is something different from original learning (Dmr, 451b). The nature of this difference is in the acquired association of impulses which, when a start is made, will lead on to recall, which cannot be the case in fully relearning (Dmr, 452a).

The activities of remembering and recalling are primarily related to different functions of the mind. Remembering is in itself an activity of the sensing power and is consequently shared by some of the irrational animals (Dmr, 450a); recalling, however, belongs only to man, since it is a kind of search in which one reasons that he has had such and such an experience before. This is possible only to man, who alone has the power of deliberation (Dmr, 453a).

Remembering, then, is in itself a function of the power of sensation, only incidentally belonging to that of thinking. What lies more closely to its essential nature is its always implying a lapse of time. When one is looking at a colored object or thinking about an object of speculative thought, he is sensing or knowing; but the persisting of this sensation or knowledge, not as an activity but as a potentiality, is remembering (Dmr, 449b).

This involvement of the factor of time, as essential to the activity of remembering, leads to another question of importance and of great difficulty: what is the character of the object of memory? Is it the affection itself, or that object from which it came to be? If it is the affect, Aristotle argues, then one could not remember absent things; but he has already established that memory is of those things which are not now objects of sensation or knowledge. But if the object of memory is the original object from which this effect came to be, how do we remember by sensing the absent, which cannot be sensed? For he has located memory in the faculty of sensation. He concludes, however, that we do just that: we see and hear what is not present. He likens the image (φάντασμα) in us to what is painted on a panel. Considered in one sense, it is a picture; in another sense it is a likeness of something—it has a reference external to itself, so to speak. Similarly with the image which is the object of memory. It can be considered in itself, and as such it is an object of mental vision (θεώρημα). It is, in the strict sense, a true object of memory only when it is considered as a likeness of something else—when it has external reference. He seems to indicate that this very difference sometimes exists when we actually sense an external object. When the response is made to what is sensed, we may be in doubt with respect to the entire nature of the situation. Are we merely sensing, or are we remembering, too? Then it sometimes happens that we recall that we have heard or seen this something before. In this case the thing arouses the response of both sensing and recalling. Considered in itself, it is an object of sensation; considered as having reference to itself as formerly sensed, it is an object of memory. In abnormal states the reverse takes place; mental pictures are taken as external things (Dmr, 450b, f.). We conclude, therefore, that remembering and recalling are the activities in which the individual responds to events which are past and to present situations in the light of experience. It is the same general pattern of power to respond to the environment which we have seen to be the key principle of Aristotle's analysis, with the environment now extended into the past, as deliberation projects it into the future.

The factors in learning which Aristotle thought to favor memory are still familiar to us. Frequency is recognized as favoring quick recall (Dmr, 452a). What we call intensity is stated in the fact that some impulses, experienced but once, are more effective in forming habits than others repeated many times (Dmr, 451b). But the most powerful factor is the association of impulses, corresponding to the succession of the original objects (Dmr, 451b, f.). This factor also suggests the effective way to recall. One should not start a general search, but should get on the track of impulses which are so associated that they will lead to the objects sought (Dmr, 451b, f.). For this reason subjects are best remembered which have an orderly arrangement, as one part naturally leads to another. Indeed the presence of this association is what makes the process of recalling different from that of learning, in which process the absence of association makes it impossible to proceed by one's own effort from point to point (Dmr, 451b, f.).

## SLEEPING AND WAKING

The activities of the organism which we have thus far considered could all be called positive. Sleep remains to be considered as something different from the mere absence of any or all of the processes which we have examined. It can be called a negative activity: negative, because its essence is partially a privation of something; an activity, because something is going on which is for a specific purpose.

Sleep and waking have reference to the same part of the living creature—sensation. They are contraries, sleep seeming to be a privation of waking. Two things constitute the essence of the waking state—the experience of sensation (Dsv, 454a) and the invariable consequent of sensation, desire (Dsv, 454b). Contrariwise, the one who sleeps does not sense; neither does he have the desire which follows sensation. However, at least in a metaphor, rest is combined with pleasure, nature's lure, so to speak, to what is beneficial (Dsv, 455b).

The unity of the organism is maintained in the description of sleep. Sensation is a movement of the soul through the body, and as the two are involved in sensation, so are they also in sleep, which is characterized by the absence of sensation (Dsv, 454a).

This definition of sleep and waking also shows the impossibility of either one continuing without interruption. Waking, involving the activity of bodily sense organs, will sooner or later result in fatigue, which will make further functioning of these parts impossible, and sleep will ensue. But sleep could not continue indefinitely, for it is not a general loss of activity, but specifically characteristic of the sensitive power; but it would not be a sensitive power if it could not sense, which is an activity of waking (Dsv, 454a, b).

Sleep is not an affection of the several senses. That would make it strange for all the senses to become inoperative simultaneously, when one or more of them were not specifically fatigued. The essential thing about sleep is not the senses being unable to sense—this happens in fainting and some mentally deranged conditions. But sleep occurs when the power of sensation itself is incapacitated: "for there is one sensation, and one paramount sense organ" (Dsv, 455a, b).

We have noted that sleep is for a purpose—the preservation of the organism. Without it, sensation could not be sustained, and sensation is necessary to thought as well. Since sensation and thinking are the end of all beings which have one or other of these capacities, sleep is essential to all living creatures (Dsv, 455b).

Sleep, then, is defined first by the absence of the critical activities of the organism and second by its function of preserving the capacities of the organism.

But if there is no activity of the critical powers, how are dreams to be explained? Dreams are not accounted for by sensation, since they occur when there is no object sensed. Yet the experience is similar to sensation, and Aristotle concludes that dreaming is related to the sensitive faculty in the same way as imagination is, calling the objects of dreaming, indeed, φαντάσματα (Ds, 458b, f.).

Opinion, in the strict sense, follows sensation, and should be impossible in dreaming. Nevertheless, there is a mental activity in dreams which goes beyond the mental pictures, in an activity similar to that which follows sensation (Ds, 458b).

Aristotle concludes that one does not sense while asleep, but that sensation is somehow affected, in a different way from that which characterizes the waking state. Opinion follows in each case, but in waking it is free to deny what appears, while in sleeping it is fettered by the mental picture (Ds, 459a).

To get an explanation of this activity during sleep, which by the rules of the game should be impossible. Aristotle turns to what goes on in waking sensory experience. He finds that there is a persistence of affection when the stimulating objects are no longer present. When we turn our eyes from the sunlight, we can see nothing because of the continuing movement in our eyes. After prolonged exposure to a color, another object to which we shift our gaze will appear similarly colored. After strong exposure to light, if the eyes are shut, the always interesting flight of colors ensues. The result of looking at moving objects will be to make objects at rest appear to be moving when we look at them (Ds, 459b). Likewise, a continuing bodily affect leads to deception of the senses by what we call "set"—the love of the lover and the fear of the coward lead to thinking that the beloved or the enemy is seen when this is not the case (Ds, 460b).

So, argues Aristotle, is it with dreams. There is a persistence of sensory affection into the sleeping state. In ordinary waking experience these persisting affects are canceled by the ongoing sensory experience; when sleep comes and they are not interfered with, they have full play as dreams (Ds, 460b, f.). However, it is possible for a man to have sufficient mental ability when asleep to be aware that he is dreaming (Ds, 462a), and it occurs, too, that faint, true sensations are experienced, such as being affected by the light of a lamp or the barking of the dogs; but these are not fully responded to, as in the waking state.

Since this true sensing and thinking, even of a limited kind, go on in sleep, we might conclude that the earlier exclusion of the critical activities was in error. Probably it would be fairer to Aristotle, however, to say that in sleep, as such, no true sensation or thinking takes place, but that in typical human experience sleep is not quite successful; there remain, therefore, the persisting of sensory affections, some true though faint sensations, and some slight processes of thought, such as opinions that follow the mental pictures and awareness that one is dreaming.

## SUMMARY

In the present chapter we have analyzed what Aristotle calls the critical functions of the soul, in distinction from the function which is responsible for causing movement. These critical activities represent various kinds of response on the part of the organism to the environment which is stimulating it. First of all, there is the establishment of working relations through sensation, which is the discrimination of the distinctions which exist in the objects of the external world. Depending upon sensation is the activity of διάνοια, or of thinking in general, which is considered under the aspects of the calculative and scientific powers. These again relate the organism to the environment, the first with respect to expediency, the second with respect to knowledge of ultimate principles for its own sake. We extended our discussion temporally by considering memory and recollection, as responding to events of the past, and examined the way in which sleeping is an activity of the organism characterized by the absence of the critical activities—with the further observation that dreams arise through the persistence of sensory affects and that some true sensation and thinking occur because sleep is not always complete.

*Chapter Five*

# METAPHYSICAL ANALYSIS OF THE LIVING BEING

IN THE preceding chapters of our study we have been occupied chiefly with the description of what goes on in the life history of an individual. The philosophic interest has never been absent. We could not discuss generation and growth without talking of such things as motion between contraries, the four causes, and necessity. We could not at all discuss the behavior of the matured individual without relating him at once to the world in which he finds himself, and which, apparently from the beginning of his life, is anything but a buzzing confusion. Nevertheless we have been primarily examining his coming-to-be, his growing, his desiring, his sensing, his knowing: "gold, and silver, and copper. Guineas, shillings, half-pence." "But what is money after all?" We now want to know more precisely just what this individual of whom we have been talking really is. What is it to be an individual? With the purpose of seeking Aristotle's answer to this question, we shall reëxamine the various doctrines which are pertinent to this inquiry.

## THE LIVING BEING

The fundamental distinctions which we meet at once are those between a body, a soul, and a living being. The body may be considered from two points of view. It may be thought of as so much matter, of a given configuration; as such, however, it is not a "natural body," although it is constituted of elements which themselves are natural things. Things which exist by nature are animals and their parts, plants, and the simple bodies, such as earth, fire, air, and water. Their distinguishing characteristic is that they have within themselves a principle of movement and rest (Ph, 192b). The living things mentioned above have this principle. In a different way the simple bodies do also; that is, what occurs to them in a given context is determined by their own characteristic ways of responding to that context, just as what occurs to a plant or an animal in a given situation is a function of its nature, considered in relation to that type of situation.

A complex body considered as so much matter, however, does not have this inner principle of movement. The dead body, although having the same pattern as the living, does not constitute the animal in question (Dpa, 640b). If the soul is not present, then flesh, or any particular part, or the animal as a whole is present only in an equivocal sense, just as they would be called such and such things, even if made of wood or stone (Dga, 734b). For it is the soul, which is the cause and first principle of the living body (Da, 415b), which constitutes the nature of an animal (Dpa, 641a). In other words, a given body is a natural body only if it has soul, which is identical with saying that what occurs to it is determined by its own principles rather than by the principles of the simple bodies which constitute its material.

The living being is therefore a distinct kind of natural phenomenon. It is not explicable in terms of matter, nor again in terms of any nonmaterial principle. It is a complexity—a product—of both. This particular, compound thing is more accessible to investigation than the elements and principles which it involves and is accordingly a basic subject matter, a starting point for inquiry (Ph, 184a). The individuals within a species are always the real existences (Dpa, 644a). In the coming-to-be of an individual, various factors are involved, but the end product is a unique thing which must be understood in terms of its own principles.

## SOUL

The term "soul" is used by Aristotle in many different ways, and our present task is to arrive at an exact notion of his fundamental doctrine of soul by analyzing the passages which give a comprehensive view of his meaning.

Fundamentally, that which has soul (*τὸ ἔμψυχον*) is distinguished from that which does not have soul (*τὸ ἄψυχον*) by living (Da, 413a). In the entire body of teaching there is an exact one-to-one correlation between the presence and absence of soul and living. The kinds of soul are differentiated in terms of the capacities of the living things themselves. Only the nutritive faculty is present in plants, and this function characterizes their soul. All other living things have not only the nutritive faculty but the sensitive as well, with appetence as the necessary consequent of sensation. These two functions are thoroughly intermingled in relating the individual to the environment in which he lives. Finally, in man, we have the culminating power of thought, which distinguishes his soul from that of all subhuman forms (Da, 414a, b). In these definitions Aristotle seeks to put content into his more general description of soul as characterizing that which lives. It is not sufficient to make such a general statement, but the particular abilities which distinguish the various classes must be stated (Da, 414b). These various gradations are necessarily arranged in a series, since the higher capacities always imply the lower. For instance, the power of thought depends upon the sensitive faculty, and that in turn upon the nutritive (Da, 415a).

Aristotle makes another approach to the meaning of "soul," which aids greatly in understanding his use of the term. It is only natural things as opposed to artificial things (Ph, 192b)—only things which have their own principle of movement—which have soul (Da, 412b). But not all such things have soul, as we have seen. In the passage cited, the division comes between one group comprising animals and their organs, and plants, and a second group comprising the elements of bodies—earth, air, fire, water. In *De anima* (412a, b) this distinction is defined. The soul is "the first actuality of a natural body potentially possessing life," and then more precisely, "the first actuality of a natural body possessed of organs."

An examination of the difference between natural bodies which have organs (which are those which live and have soul) and those which do not, leads to a clearer understanding of Aristotle's exact meaning when he uses the term "soul." In the case of natural bodies which do not have organs, movement is explicable in terms of the character of the element itself, which is identical with the body. On the other hand, the movement of those natural bodies which have organs is explicable only in terms of (1) function: an organ implies use, differentiated from the use of other organs; and (2) individuality: an organ implies some whole thing of which it is the instrument. Therefore, since soul is that which distinguishes natural things which have organs from those which do not, and since the functioning of organs as instruments of an individual is what makes the distinction, soul is the total activity of such a complex, integral thing.

Aristotle's illustrations further confirm this interpretation. If the eye were a living being, its soul would be its seeing. This is analogous to the case of the whole living body. Just as the pupil and the power of seeing constitute the eye, so the body and soul constitute the living being (Da, 413a). A body is, without doubt, defined by its potentialities. Similarly, each kind of soul can exist only in its own kind of body, rather than being connected with any kind of body. Why? Because the actuality of each particular thing belongs to the potentiality of that particular thing (Da, 414a). In this passage it is implied that the soul is identical with the activity of the body, for it is the actuality of a body of a given potentiality. This is in accord with what we have repeatedly seen to be the case in defining the various kinds of souls. In each case the soul is defined in terms of certain powers, of which it is also the first principle (Da, 413b). These are powers of the individual to act in determinate ways. This fact expresses the further meaning of "soul" as representing not alone the activity of the individual but the potentiality for that activity. This is why the soul is the *first* actuality of a natural body having organs, Aristotle in this way acknowledging soul to be identical with the potentialities of the organism rather than with its activities alone, just as we have seen that the various "parts" of the soul have potentialities or actualized existence according to whether or not they are functioning: such as the mind (νοῦς), which is actualized only in thinking.

This doctrine of Aristotle has been expressed in so many ways in this discussion because it is very difficult to apprehend as an activity something which is talked about in substantive terms. Aristotle seems to have experienced the same difficulty, if not in understanding his own doctrine, at least in expressing it! This is perhaps nowhere shown so instructively as in a passage which discusses the soul's relation to the various parts of the body.

> And the animal organism must be conceived after the similitude of a well-governed commonwealth. When order is once established in it there is no more need of a separate monarch to preside over each several task. The individuals each play their assigned part as it is ordered, and one thing follows another in its accustomed order. So in animals there is the same orderliness—nature taking the place of custom—and each part naturally doing his own work as nature has composed them. There is no need then of a soul in each part, but she resides in a kind of central governing place of the body, and the remaining parts live by continuity of natural structure, and play the parts Nature would have them play [Dma, 703a, b].

Great care is needed in the interpretation of such a highly figurative passage. But if we make full use of what we have discovered in more technical statements, this figure gives a beautiful picture of Aristotle's doctrine of the living being. We have seen how the parts of the soul—the various aspects of its total function—are functions which involve the parts of the body. The soul is the function of the entire body, but Aristotle is saying in this figurative way that the total function is something quite different from the sum of the various functions. A man's little finger is a vital part of him, but, if the finger is cut off, there is a sense in which the man himself is undiminished. There is a wholeness, an integrity of the soul of every individual which cannot quite be described by the catalog of his separable functions. But it is not that a man possesses this integral soul *and* the parts: he rather possesses (or more precisely is constituted by) an integral soul which *involves* parts.

## THE RELATION OF SOUL AND BODY

With the view which Aristotle takes that the soul is the function of a living body, the question of the relation of soul and body in its usual form has already been settled. There remains, however, a kind of relation which has frequently engaged our attention in the course of this study and which is pertinent to our present interest.

To get a right view of the distinctions which are involved in this relation, the question may be restated: "What are the different relations of the soul, in its various aspects, to the *material* of the body?" The answer to this question, in turn, is found to be correlative to the answer to a second question: "What are the different relations of the living being, with respect to his defining functions, to the environing world?"

The most general function of the soul is the nutritive, and we shall begin with it. Nutrition implies an environment which has a definite effect upon the organism. The distinguishing character of this effect is that material is taken into the body (Da, 424a, b). A red, sweet, winy apple will nourish the organism; but color, taste, and smell will not.

The sensitive function of the soul involves activity of a more complex nature. It is exclusively the response of a natural body, but a body which, considered in this aspect, has the capacity to respond to the form of external objects without being acted upon by their matter. Two things have happened in this step from the nutritive to the sensitive powers of the soul. First, the environment has been vastly enlarged and diversified. In many more respects there exist powers of the organism to be affected by the environment, in both the sensory experiences themselves and in the appetence which is aroused through sensation. Second, the nature of the environmental effect upon the organism is formal, rather than material. This means that objects stimulate the organism and arouse response without immediate contact. The environment and the organism can at once be indefinitely distant from each other and immediately present.

A third step is taken when we come to the rational powers of the soul. It is very clear, as we have seen, that the functions of the mind depend upon the activities of sense. At the same time, they go beyond sensory experience, especially in the actualization of universals. We are discussing the relations of the living being to the environing world from the standpoint of an inquiry into the relation of soul and body, and in this speculative activity of the mind we have reached the function of the soul, which, while depending on the activity of the body, nevertheless explores the completely immaterial—pure forms. Since there must be similarity in character between the receiver and the received, this implies the immateriality of the soul in its power of dealing with universals, or, in other words, in its power to see (θεωρεῖν) the essential nature of things. Aristotle accordingly talks of the theoretical power of the soul as separable, as the eternal is separable from the perishable (Da, 413b). It is, when acting, unmixed in its essence, and not acted upon. That does not mean, however, that in this case the soul acts upon the environment rather than being acted upon by it; rather, the two become one, for knowledge, functioning, is identical with its object (Da, 430a). This is why the soul, considered under this aspect, is in a sense the entire universe (Da, 431b).

To sum up: with Aristotle's definition of the soul as the actuality of a natural body having organs, the usual problem of the relation of soul and body does not exist. There remains, however, another question, which involves the analysis of the living being into the factors of body and soul: what is the relation of the living being to the environing world? The answer to this question is not found in one formula, but in examining the specific functions of the soul with respect to the relations which each one involves. This examination yields an ascending scale, from the nutritive function of the soul, and its concern with the material of the environment, to the power of speculative thought, which deals with pure form. All these powers are operative in man, so that the human soul functions with respect to purely material concerns, receives the forms of material objects, and in its highest capacity becomes identified with the intelligible world.

## THE QUESTION OF PERMANENCE

It is strange that any doubt exists with regard to Aristotle's position on the mortality or immortality of the soul. The difficulty arises through considering the soul as the primary thing to be inquired into. That necessarily leads into devious paths of controversy. But it is perfectly plain from Aristotle himself that the living being is the primary object of his inquiry. The soul is distinguished as a kind of multiple factor in the behavior of this individual, and we can therefore be prepared to receive a plural answer to any question which we may address to it.

Aristotle definitely teaches that the individual perishes. Even in a passage (Da, 408b) which speaks of the imperishability of the mind, he shows also that activities such as remembering and loving fail because the man fails; they are part of the complex being which perishes. Indeed he believes this to be a necessary implication of his entire view of the nature of living things. It is impossible for living beings to be everlasting as individuals, although they are so as species (Dga, 731b), and this belief is based on the fact that the substance (οὐσία) of living beings is perishable (Dgc, 338b). Aristotle makes the desire to share in the immortal and divine the basis of the instinct of reproduction, for every creature strives for this. . . . Since, then, they cannot share in the immortal and divine by continuity of existence, because no perishable thing can remain numerically one and the same, they share in these in the only way they can. . . . What persists is not the individual itself, but something in its image, not identical as a unit, but identical in form [Da, 415b].

It is Aristotle's treatment of νοῦς which has given rise to various interpretations of his doctrine of mortality. It seems to have some existence of its own and not to suffer decay (Da, 408b). In its true nature it is separated, deathless, eternal (Da, 430a). But we have seen that when this mind is operating, it is identical with its object—it is thus not a purely personal, individual matter, but is the intelligible order of the world in which the man as a whole participates while he is a living being.

There is a beautiful passage in Plato's *Phaedo* which presents a doctrine of generation from contraries, which, in its contrast to Aristotle's, illuminates what Aristotle means by the immortality of νοῦς. Socrates is arguing with his friends that it is better for him to leave the body and he establishes the view of immortality by the fact that all things which come to be, do so from their contraries. Then when a human being comes into life, what is it from which he comes? From death, life's contrary. But how did that being come into death? From life, death's contrary. There is a ceaseless recurrence, and therefore Socrates knows that he will not utterly perish when he drinks the hemlock at evening.

It is aside from our purpose to indulge in the exercise of interpreting what Plato actually meant to convey in this language. What is essential for us is that in this view the soul is immortal, in just the same way in which it was preexistent. That is, it is eternal. Now that is how Aristotle talks about νοῦς. It is immortal, in the same way in which it was preëxistent. It is eternal and divine. But he consistently identifies this with the totality of the intelligible world and allows it to man only as the most highly prized possession of an individual, who belongs to the order of things which come to be and which pass away.

### SUMMARY

What, then, is the living being, who is the subject of inquiry in psychology? Aristotle's doctrine may be summarized by saying that he is a generated, perishable thing. His coming-to-be and his entire existence are the product of various factors which may be subsumed under the terms body and soul. It is his soul which constitutes his essential nature, and its analysis shows it to be the activity of the individual, considered as an organic whole. On every level of living, and increasingly so as higher capacities come into view, this activity is understood in terms of determinate potentialities of the organism, actualized by the stimulation of the environment. The soul is thus a joint function of both the organism and its environment, a last connecting link between the unmoved mover and this moved being, the fusion point of the individual and the whole of Nature, and yet a unity in all this plurality. If it is difficult for us to assign an ontological status to such a thing as the soul which Aristotle describes, the difficulty springs from our being unaccustomed to include temporal factors in our view of reality, and for Aristotle neither a living being nor his soul can be defined apart from his history.

# APPENDIX: ANALYTICAL OUTLINE OF "THE PSYCHOLOGY"

## CHAPTER ONE. THE GENERATION OF THE ORGANISM

### *Introduction*

The organism belongs to the kind of natural things which are subject to generation and decay, so that the first subject for investigation is its generation.

There was no place for genuine coming-to-be and passing-away in the doctrines of the monists and pluralists who preceded Aristotle.

Plato's treatment of the subject was inadequate.

There are two aspects of the general problem of development.

### *Distinctions Involved in the Explanation of Generation*

Concrete things are the starting point of investigation in natural philosophy.

The character of these things is always related to their environment.

The development which is to be explained appears as a passage from the potential to the actual.

Coming-to-be and passing-away take place in the field of contraries.

The agent and patient in coming-to-be are described in terms of presence and absence of a given form.

Summary.

### *The Senses in Which Psyche Is a Factor in Generation*

In organisms psyche functions as the final, formal, and efficient causes.

Psyche is a factor in the generation and development of organisms.

It characterizes the body from the beginning of the embryo.

The male and female principles contribute in different ways to generation.

### *The Significance of Aristotle's Doctrine of Development*

## CHAPTER TWO. THE GROWTH OF THE ORGANISM

### *Introduction*

Three kinds of activity are involved in the growth of the initiated organism: nutrition, increase, and differentiation and maturation of the parts.

### *Nutrition*

That which is assimilated is determined by the character of that which assimilates.

### *Increase*

Increase is a movement between contraries.

It is the whole organism which increases.

There are three distinctive marks of increase.

Form and matter are distinguished in increase.

A part increases by that which has the potentiality of becoming that part.

Increase takes place in accordance with an active principle.

That which comes-to-be in increase is not quantity-in-general but flesh or bone.

### *Differentiation and Maturation of the Parts*

Introduction: Aristotle makes use of the comparative method; he insists that explanatory principles must not be general, but specific to the subject-matter.

The fundamental causes of differentiation are two: (1) the parts are potentially present in the material; (2) the principle of movement is imparted by the male, which causes the serial development of the parts.

Final cause and heredity are different ways of viewing the development of typical characters.

Heredity

The characters which will eventuate in the offspring are determined by the seed, which has formative properties.

The embryo and semen have soul potentially but not actually.

Parent-child resemblance in developed organs is caused by the semen determining the development of similar heart and blood.

Variations from parental pattern result from failure of the semen to master the material.

Sex is determined by the quality of the heart.

Characters common to a class differ from those which vary among individuals.

Final Cause

An artistic spirit designed even the humbler animals.

A key-principle in design is "elegance."

Final cause is first.

It is involved in that which constitutes a body what it is, and is internal to that body.

Psyche functions as final cause.

Man's rational superiority corresponds to his superiority of requisite organs.

The activity which is caused by heredity and final cause takes place in accordance with necessity.

The teleological type of activity which yet occurs by necessity is controlled by the end to be achieved.

Physiological resources determine order of development.

These physiological resources are furnished in a sequence according to function.

Capacities and organs develop synchronously.

Growth involves activity in a comprehensive sequence.

There are three degrees of composition.

The order of development is the inverse of the order of logical existence.

The whole form is in the embryo.
The parts are developed in an order of priority.
Homogeneous parts exist for the sake of the heterogeneous.
The order of development is from the general to the particular, from the internal to the external.
Not only the organism as a whole but each part develops from mass to differentiated form.
A question of great difficulty is when, how, and whence reason is acquired.

Some parts are themselves principles.
Psyche functions as efficient cause.

## CHAPTER THREE. THE INITIATION AND CONTROL OF BEHAVIOR

### *Introduction*

Psychology in Aristotle's terms primarily concerns behavior.

### *Mind and Appetence Distinguished*

Two things characterize that which has soul: (1) movement and (2) sensibility.
Parts of the soul refer to functions which can be separately discussed.
Neither the nutritive function of the soul, nor the sensitive, nor the rational, is responsible in itself for movement.

### *Appetence Described in Terms of Interaction Between the Organism and Its Environment*

Three things are to be considered: (1) the moving cause, (2) the means by which it produces movement, and (3) the thing moved.
Appetence is thus the intermediate factor between the external goal and the moved organism.

### *The Practical Mind Involved with Appetence in Producing Movement*

It is distinguished from the speculative mind by having an end in view.

The end to be achieved is the starting point of the practical mind.

The action of the practical mind may be schematized as syllogistic reasoning.

Ideomotor activity is the rule if nothing hinders.

*Appetence and the Four Causes*

The question arises, can the motivating power of appetence be analyzed in terms of the four causes, or does Aristotle here deal with causation of a completely different order?

What the analysis into parts is to the body of an organism, the analysis of activity is to the form.

The analysis of activity reveals the form of an organism as having two complementary characters: (1) it is internally dynamic, and (2) it is environmentally stimulated; appetence is a term used in describing such activity and involves no new kind of causal factor.

*The Operation of Appetence*

Natural functions are pleasant, and an organism strives for what is pleasant.

The relation between the organism and its environment involved in an "affection of the soul" is expressed in saying that the latter is an idea which is "enmattered."

Pleasure is a reaction of the entire living being which does not have the specific kind of context in which an affection typically appears.

Conflicting ends complicate the operation of appetence.

Mind is involved in activity in various ways: (1) in projecting a conflicting future end, (2) in directing activity, (3) in delaying it.

A voluntary act is one whose origin is within the agent.

Intelligent response (προαίρεσις) is a special kind of voluntary act.

It takes place after deliberation, and is identical with the result of deliberation.

The analysis of intelligent response is the basis for conclusions about man's capacity to determine his own actions.

***Summary on the Factors Which Are Involved in the Initiation and Control of Behavior***

## CHAPTER FOUR. THE CRITICAL ACTIVITIES OF THE ORGANISM

### *Introduction*

The activities of an organism are instrumental to its satisfaction.
Sensing and thinking are the two functions of the critical capacity.

### *Sensing as the First Activity of the Organism Aroused by the Environment*

Sensation is the most essential of the capacities which imply the presence of life.
It is directly related to appetence.
It is a function of the environment and consequently has, in itself, only potential existence.
It is an experience of the individual by means of specialized organs.
The stimulus of sensation is always a particular object, of one of three kinds. The difference between sensation and perception is analyzed in terms of the object sensed rather than in the activity itself.
The stimulus comes through a medium.
The various senses are considered with respect to their objects, media, and organs: (1) vision, (2) hearing, (3) smell, (4) taste, (5) touch.
Common sensibles are sensed not by a special sense organ, but by common sensation.
The objects of different senses can be judged different because of the unity of the judging capacity.
Awareness of sensation arises with the first sense.
Summary on the nature of sensation.

### *Thinking as the Critical Activity of the Organism Which Has to Do with the Nature or Forms of Things in the External World*

It is distinguished from sensing.
It participates with appetence in producing movement.

The mind has actual existence only when thinking.

The forms which are objects of thought differ from the forms of sensible objects.

There is a unity in the thinking which occurs in the universe, grounded in the one order of particular things in nature.

Error occurs in both sensing and thinking.

The various aspects of the activity of mind are analyzed in terms of:

1. The calculative power, the activity of which is characterized by the two excellences (1) art, and (2) practical intelligence, and is analyzed as (1) imagination, (2) grasping, (3) opinion, (4) calculation, (5) deliberation, and (6) intelligent response.
2. The scientific power, the activity of which is characterized by the three excellences (1) scientific knowledge, (2) theoretical intelligence, and (3) wisdom, and is analyzed as (1) grasping, (2) knowing (in different senses), (3) conviction, (4) learning, and (5) beholding.

Summary on the activities of thinking.

*The Past Involved in the Behavior of the Organism, in and Through Its Activities of Remembering and Recalling*

Remembering is an activity of the sensing power, recalling is of the thinking.

A difficult question is, "Is the object of memory the present affect in the mind, or that object from which it came to be?"

The factors in learning which favor memory are frequency, intensity, and association of impulses.

*Sleep as a Negative Activity Having Reference to the Power of Sensing*

It is impossible for sleep or waking to continue without interruption.

Sleep is defined by the absence of the critical activities and by its function of preserving the organism's capacities.

Dreams are explained in terms of persisting sensory affections, some true though faint sensations, and some slight processes of thought.

*Summary on the Critical Activities of the Organism*

## CHAPTER FIVE. METAPHYSICAL ANALYSIS OF THE LIVING BEING

*Introduction*

The question of the chapter is, "What is it to be an individual?"

*The Living Being as a Concrete Whole or Individual, Analyzed in Terms of Body and Soul*

*Analysis of "Soul"*

The term is used by Aristotle in different ways.
- It distinguishes the living from the non-living.
- The kinds of soul are differentiated in terms of the capacities of living things: (a) the nutritive, (b) the sensitive, and (c) the rational.

A second approach aids in understanding the term "soul."
- It characterizes only natural as opposed to artificial things, and only such natural things as have organs.
- Natural things which have organs are distinguished from those which do not in terms of (a) differentiated functions and (b) individuality.

Aristotle's different approaches and illustrations reveal his view of soul as the total activity—considered as potential or actual—of a complex, integral organism.

*The Relation of Soul and Body*

The question may be reduced to "What are the different relations of the living being to the environing world?"

The answer is considered with respect to the defining functions of the living being.

*The Question of Permanence*

The answer depends on what is being considered: the living being, his soul, or a part of his soul.

*Summary on the Metaphysical Analysis of the Living Being*

# INDEX

Bei Fragen zur Produktsicherheit wenden Sie sich bitte an:
If you have any questions regarding product safety,
please contact:

Walter de Gruyter GmbH
Genthiner Straße 13
10785 Berlin
productsafety@degruyterbrill.com